The Consolidation of
Democracy in Latin America

GERARDO OTERO
OCTUBRE, 1995
VANCOUVER

Woodrow Wilson Center
Current Studies on Latin America

Published with the Latin American Program
of the Woodrow Wilson International Center for Scholars
Joseph S. Tulchin, Director

The Consolidation
of Democracy in
Latin America

edited by
Joseph S. Tulchin
with Bernice Romero

LYNNE
RIENNER
PUBLISHERS

BOULDER
LONDON

Published in the United States of America in 1995 by
Lynne Rienner Publishers, Inc.
1800 30th Street, Boulder, Colorado 80301

and in the United Kingdom by
Lynne Rienner Publishers, Inc.
3 Henrietta Street, Covent Garden, London WC2E 8LU

Library of Congress Cataloging-in-Publication Data
The consolidation of democracy in Latin America / edited by Joseph S.
  Tulchin with Bernice Romero.
  (Woodrow Wilson Center current studies on Latin
  America)
  Includes bibliographical references and index.
  ISBN 1-55587-607-2 (alk. paper)
    1. Democracy—Latin America—Congresses. 2. Latin America—
2. Democracy—Peru—Congresses. 3. Peru—Economic conditions—1980–
Economic policy—Congresses. I. Tulchin, Joseph S., 1939– .
II. Romero, Bernice. III. Series.
JL966.C675 1995
338.98'009'049—dc20   95-17928
                                                              CIP

British Cataloguing in Publication Data
A Cataloguing in Publication record for this book
is available from the British Library.

Printed and bound in the United States of America

       The paper used in this publication meets the requirements
  ∞   of the American National Standard for Permanence of
       Paper for Printed Library Materials Z39.48-1984.

    5 4 3 2 1

Contents

Foreword

That the overwhelming majority of the countries in Latin America have democratically elected governments for the first time in history should be understood as a significant achievement, but not as a guarantee of a democratic future for the region. This idea led the directors of the Olof Palme International Foundation to propose focusing its Third International Forum on the elements required to make possible the consolidation of democracy in Latin America.

The crisis in Eastern Europe, which began in 1989, effectively put an end to the models of popular democracy and the planned state economy and precipitated a fundamental change in international relations—which to that point had been based on division of the world into two great blocs that operated within the framework of the Cold War, defined by the bipolar logic that dominated not only international relations but domestic politics as well.

We lived through a period of four decades in which the world was thus divided into two areas of mutually exclusive loyalties, opposed principles of sociopolitical organization, and economies in which the mode of production and incentives were based on very different assumptions. For their part, domestic politics in Latin America were constrained by this framework in which anti-communism, and with it the explicit alliance with one of the superpowers under the terms of the Cold War, was raised repeatedly as an excuse to oppose any kind of social reform.

Today, the democratization of Latin America is a reality. Nevertheless, complicated problems resulting from debt, misery, and social injustice continue to exist and give rise to a nostalgia for authoritarianism. The compelling need to consolidate the fragile democracies in the region points to the importance of a just distribution of wealth and effective external aid.

It has been a great pleasure for the Olof Palme International Foundation to organize the forum jointly with the Woodrow Wilson International Center for Scholars and to prepare this English-language edition of the papers presented there. The original Spanish version was presented to the public on December 19, 1994, at the headquarters of the foundation in Badalona, Spain, by José Luis Dicenta, secretary of state for international cooperation and Latin America of the Spanish Ministry of Foreign Affairs, and by Joseph S. Tulchin, director of the Wilson Center Latin American Program and director of the Third International Forum.

We recognize that some time has elapsed since the forum was held in 1993. For that reason we asked the authors of these chapters to revise the papers originally presented at the forum and to bring their reflections and observations up to date. We continue to be interested in the consolidation of democracy in Latin America and look forward to future collaboration with the Woodrow Wilson Center on this and other issues of significance to the region.

Anna Balletbó
Secretary General of the
Olof Palme International Foundation

Preface

This book originated in conversations I had with Anna Balletbó during her stay at the Woodrow Wilson Center in 1992 as a fellow. Her interest in Latin America and my interest in Spain created the basis for animated exchanges. We shared the firm conviction that Latin America had a long way to go on the road toward consolidated democracy and that Spain's interest in the region should be expressed in some concrete, academic manner. It was during these conversations that Anna invited me to organize the International Forum on Latin America for the Olof Palme International Foundation. The foundation and the Wilson Center shared the expense and the effort required to put on the forum in Badalona, Spain, in January 1993. The foundation published the papers from that forum, in Spanish, at the end of 1994.

Because the issues raised during the forum appear even more significant today than they did then, we decided to ask the authors of those papers to update their work with a view to making them less vulnerable to the passage of time. For that reason we have left out of this publication several presentations that referred principally to Spain or Spanish policies at the time of the forum. We hope that this volume will be of use to Latin Americanists in a wide range of disciplines because it deals with the central issues of concern to contemporary Latin America—economic development, political consolidation, social equity and unrest, and international relations.

* * *

I want to take this opportunity to thank Anna Balletbó and her able staff, which for a time included my son, Andrew Tulchin, for their splendid support in planning and coordinating the forum. The bulk of the work in preparing this manuscript for publication was performed by Bernice Romero, who at the time was program associate in the Latin American Program at the Woodrow Wilson Center. Bernice also helped me draft the Introduction. Ralph Espach assisted me in the final stages of publication. I am grateful, also, to the authors of the various chapters who were generous with their time in revising their original submissions. Obviously, they share my belief that these are important issues.

Joseph S. Tulchin
Director, Latin American Program
Woodrow Wilson International Center for Scholars

Introduction

Joseph S. Tulchin with Bernice Romero

In January 1993, the Latin American Program of the Woodrow Wilson International Center, in conjunction with the Olof Palme International Foundation, sponsored a forum, "Democratic Consolidation in Latin America," in Badalona, Spain. In keeping with the Latin American Program's objective to promote dialogue and exchange regarding pressing contemporary issues in the region, the forum brought together prominent scholars and specialists in the study of democracy to examine the topics and challenges of most importance to democratic consolidation in Latin America.

Participants began by clarifying two premises that are often confused in discussions about Latin America. First, it is important to remember that the region is far from uniform, and that generalizations about the twenty or more countries (more than thirty if the anglophone Caribbean is included) must be handled with extreme care. Second, the transitions in the region have occurred at different times, at different speeds, and with different components. In addition to making these clarifications, it was also agreed that economic restructuring programs would be discussed only as they impinged directly on the consolidation of democracy.

This book comes out of that forum. The selected essays that comprise the volume's eight chapters represent the main currents of the discussion that took place. The consolidation of democracy in Latin America was examined from three perspectives: obstacles to the democratization process, the political consequences of economic reform programs, and the external context for democratization.

Joseph S. Tulchin is director of the Latin American Program of the Woodrow Wilson Center. Bernice Romero is former program associate in the Latin American Program.

1

The Chapters

Philippe Schmitter begins the collection by taking a general view, outlining nine reflections to guide the study of democratic consolidation: (1) Democracy is not inevitable and it is revocable. As a result, democracies require continuous maintenance and there is always a threat of subsequent "deconsolidation." (2) Transitions from autocratic or authoritarian regimes can lead to diverse outcomes. (3) It is not democracy that is being consolidated, but one or another type of democracy. (4) The type of democracy will depend on the mode of transition from autocracy, because the transition period establishes the context in which arrangements for future cooperation and competition as well as power relations are determined. (5) Each type of democracy has its own way of consolidating itself—has its own rhythm and sequence. (6) At this time in history, democracy is the only legitimate model of political domination. But although new democracies will try to adopt and modify the experiences of established liberal democracies, they do so under very different domestic and international conditions. (7) Transitions to democracy rarely occur in isolation. They inherit accumulated demands and processes of socioeconomic and cultural change. (8) Democracies tend to emerge in waves. Each new case contributes to the generation of formal and informal organizations and networks whose claims affect the structure of democracy and often reinforce a trend away from returning to autocracy. (9) It is possible to move from autocracy to democracy without fulfilling prerequisites that theorists once held to be indispensable (e.g., revolution or civil war, popular mobilization, a high level of economic development, the existence of a national bourgeoisie, or of a civic culture, or of many democrats). These conditions may be desirable and conducive to democratic stability, but they are not necessary.

Schmitter concludes by reiterating that democracy is a choice, not a necessity, demanding continuous effort and maintenance because of the complex processes of cooperation and competition upon which it depends. He predicts that although the present wave of regime changes will leave behind more numerous and widely distributed examples of democracy, some will revert to autocracy. In addition, a deep source of disillusionment (*desencanto*) will ensue as modern democracy fails to address many social and political inequalities.

It is this sense of desencanto that occupies Parts 2 and 3 of this volume. In Chapter 2, "Democracy and the Metaphor of Good Government," Edelberto Torres Rivas looks at the concept of "good government" as a metaphor for the policies, procedures, and decisions that put public office in the service of social justice for the majority. Although recognizing that fair elections have been held, and the importance of these elections, Torres Rivas points to the weaknesses and corruption of many of the ensuing civilian governments. Corruption in Brazil, attempted coups in Guatemala and Venezuela, the successful *autogolpe* in Peru, and alliances between drug cartels and government officials in South America are cited as evidence of failed attempts to consolidate a democratic system—a system responding to popular demands for social equality and political participation. According to Torres Rivas, Latin America faces the challenge of legitimizing public authority, not merely by holding elections but by ensuring citizen participation in political processes and by showing an equal level of commitment to social policies as to policies promoting economic growth. The public must have a minimum of confidence in political institutions and in the potential for a better future. This confidence will be obtained only if leaders address social problems, thereby legitimizing their authority and reinforcing democratic consolidation.

A more specific analysis of politicians' accountability to the electorate is found in Susan Stokes's chapter, "Democracy and the Limits of Popular Sovereignty in South America." Stokes begins by stating a basic premise for the desirability and superiority of democratic systems: in a democracy people are sovereign. This sovereignty relies on representation, which in turn depends on electoral accountability. Elections indicate voters' policy preferences and thus serve as a mechanism for transmitting interests and preferences of civil society into the policymaking process. Yet Stokes's examination of five cases —Menem's 1989 election in Argentina, Fujimori's 1990 victory in Peru, Borja's 1988 victory in Ecuador, Durán's 1992 victory in Ecuador, and Paz Estenssoro's 1985 election in Bolivia. Each example showed that the general policy orientation expressed by winning candidates in their electoral campaigns was not the same as the policy orientation implemented once their governments were in power. In four of the five cases, the new governments imposed economic policies that were radically different from those they proposed during their campaigns. In fact, policies often reflected the platforms of the candidates that had been defeated.

Stokes argues that pressure exerted by domestic and international elites, combined with uncertainty regarding the potential success of any set of policies and perceived voter manipulability lead to a dangerous policy shift that constitutes a tension between popular sovereignty and dependent capitalism.

In Chapter 4, "Building Citizenship: A Balance Between Solidarity and Responsibility," Elizabeth Jelin turns away from the focus on government to analyze the rights and responsibilities of the governed. Jelin notes that the concept of citizenship is rooted in the definition of rights and obligations that constitute it. According to Jelin, the process of learning rights and responsibilities takes place in specific institutional frameworks that must be built or rebuilt in periods of transition to democracy. As state and civil institutions are restructured, the recognition and enforcement of citizens' rights are altered. Politicians have to take into account the rights and identities of different social participants. In turn, citizens must adopt beliefs and behaviors that are compatible with democracy and the new institutional system. However, the structuring of institutions and the building of a democratic political culture is complicated because the responsibilities of the state and those of the citizenry are unclear during transition periods. The citizens have the right and responsibility of demanding, promoting, and policing the democratization of the state at a time when they are still learning and building citizenship within a democratic framework. Effectively creating democratic institutions depends on the capacity of civil organizations to transform citizen-state relations. Jelin refers to human rights organizations as an example of how a third party can publicize and legitimize a cause, thereby questioning the legitimacy of the state and holding it accountable. In Latin America, Jelin argues, social movements and civil organizations can follow this model and monitor the transformation of state-citizen relations.

Part 3 of the book, "The Problems and Consequences of Economic Reform," opens with Moisés Naím's "New Competitive Tigers or Old Populist Nationalisms?" Naím analyzes domestic factors that will influence Latin American countries' foreign policies. The main concern of Latin American governments, Naím argues, will be to consolidate economic reforms even as they deepen the processes of democratization. Naím outlines four basic insufficiencies that increase the difficulty of this task and that will help shape future domestic and foreign policies. They are: (1) The social deficit. Increased poverty and inequalities has led to the need to identify policies and programs that will allow more equally distributed income. (2) The institutional deficit. Public agencies must be able to implement more effective social policies. In order for this to be achieved, the state's institutional capacity must increase. (3) The democratic deficit: transitions to democracy in many cases have increased the power and influence of legislatures, judiciaries, and governments; they have lessened the dependency of the private sector on the government, and increased the independence and power of the media. It has also led to increased demands for political participation and a rejection of traditional parties and politicians. This has resulted in governments with small majorities, unclear mandates, and widely diversified power structures that weaken the state's capacity for policy enforcement. (4) The investment deficit. Investment in infrastructure as well as human resources has been neglected to the point that Latin America may be unable to compete with other countries for investments from governments, multilateral agencies, and the industrial complex.

In the future, Latin America will focus on increased competitiveness in the international market. To meet these objectives, economic integration within and outside of the region will become a primary tool of international relations. Naím expects to see a growing stratification of Latin American countries' ability to compete in the global economy. Greater competitiveness would allow any given country to deal more effectively with its deficit, but this will largely depend on the quality of the country's leadership.

Osvaldo Sunkel's chapter, "Economic Reform and Democratic Viability," gives an overview of the democratic waves that have rolled over Latin America since World War II. The first wave, in the middle of this century, (1940s–1970s), he points out, was characterized by an expanded state role in the productive and social sectors. During this period, the economies of Latin America experienced unprecedented growth rates and the state was able to serve as the generating force behind economic development. Sunkel tracks the system as it came into crisis in the 1960s, when international borrowing allowed countries to ignore the growing balance of payments and public sector deficits. The debt crisis of 1982 forced Latin American countries to implement neoliberal economic policies that could correct the structural imbalances accumulated during the previous period. Sunkel argues, however, that the disproportionate impact of such policies on the working and middle classes constitutes a threat to democratic stability. While recognizing that economic restructuring is necessary and inevitable, Sunkel argues that more moderate and less socially devastating measures should be explored. Policies should be formulated whose positive and negative impact is more equally distributed among the social sectors.

The book's final section, Part 4, "Latin American Democracies in the International Context," turns to the implications of democracy in Latin America for the region's international role. In Chapter 7, "Changing Paradigms in Latin America: From Dependency to Neoliberalism in the International Context," Juan Gabriel Valdes focuses on changes in the ideological paradigms and perceptions that have defined Latin America's international role in the past. The current integrationist trend in the region constitutes a break from the prevailing notions of Latin America as a victim of the international system. Far from isolationist and revolutionary, Latin American national interests are defined as achieving competitive integration into the global economy. Problems of poverty and social marginalization are to be addressed, not by revolution or protectionism but by economic growth, job creation, and increased education. The question remains whether a neoliberal paradigm will be sufficient to address Latin America's social problems. Valdes emphasizes that, although the shift may be necessary in the global context, it is not in itself a solution to the region's poverty. In fact, he points to pitfalls such as a discrediting of state action in areas of assistance, education, and health at a time when increased poverty and marginalization threatens democratic stability.

Valdes goes on to address Latin America's attempts to enter the global marketplace. While the cold war once defined the parameters and nature of US–Latin American relations, new subjects now define hemispheric policy—for example, trade, immigration, and drugs. As Latin American economies diversify their markets and increase their proportion of manufactured goods, they will need to revise the integration of their market with that of the United States and find new areas of mutual interest and benefit. Conditions are now more favorable for economic integration within Latin America. But there is a widening gap between countries in economic competitiveness and a few competitive economies may bear the burden of growth for the region.

In the final chapter, "The United States and Latin America in Today's World," Joseph Tulchin examines changes in US policy toward Latin America. Tulchin argues that the decline of the cold war and its influence on hemispheric relations resulted in the diminished importance of Latin America in the eyes of US policymakers. While the United States may have maintained a salient international role, its policies in Latin America have centered on (and have often been limited to) trade and economic relations. US policy in the region today is based on avoiding involvement unless domestic policies make that impossible. In defining its international role, Latin America must bear in mind this new relation to the United States and come to terms with the liberalization of world trade and the growing globalization of capital, information, and technology. In an increasingly competitive international economy, Latin America will need to find niches in which it can compete with other producers, and to gain access to and attract technology. The region must also devote more resources to improving the competitiveness of its labor force.

The United States will continue to be the unrivalled hegemonic power in the hemisphere, and Latin America will receive relatively little attention. This, however, may afford Latin America a historical opportunity to exercise autonomy in the definition of its role in world affairs and in determining the nature of the new national security agenda.

This book provides valuable insights into the challenges and opportunities facing the region as the countries of Latin America attempt to consolidate the institutions and processes that will ensure continued democracy.

PART 1

THE TRANSITION TO DEMOCRACY

1

Transitology: The Science or the Art of Democratization?

Philippe C. Schmitter

Not so long ago, at the first conference I attended in Eastern Europe on democratization, a distinguished Hungarian sociologist introduced me to the audience as "that well-known transitologist." I felt like Monsieur Jourdan in Molière's *Le Bourgeois Gentilhomme:* enormously pleased to learn that I had been speaking prose all along without knowing it. There I was, a renowned expert in a scientific discipline the very existence of which I had just learned.

This proto- and, perhaps, pseudoscience would explain and, hopefully, guide the way from an autocratic to a democratic regime. Its founder and patron saint, if it has one, would be Niccolò Machiavelli. The so-called wily Florentine was the first great political theorist, not only to treat political outcomes as the artifactual and contingent product of human collective action, but also to recognize the specific problematics and dynamics of regime change. Machiavelli, of course, was preoccupied with change in the inverse direction—from republican to princely regimes—but his basic insights remain valid.[1]

Machiavelli gave to transitology its fundamental principle: *uncertainty;* he also formulated its first and most important maxim:

> There is nothing more difficult to execute, nor more dubious of success, nor more dangerous to administer than to introduce a new system of things: for he who introduces it has all those who profit from the old system as his enemies and he has only lukewarm allies in all those who might profit from the new system.

Furthermore, Machiavelli warned us that the potential contribution of the discipline would always be modest. According to his estimate,

Philippe C. Schmitter is professor of political science at Stanford University.

11

"in female times" (i.e., during periods when actors behaved capriciously, immorally, and without benefit of shared rules) only 50 percent of political events were understandable. The other half were due to unpredictable events, to *fortuna*.

Hence was transitology born (and promptly forgotten), with limited scientific pretensions and marked practical concerns. At best, it was doomed to become a complex mixture of rules of invariable political behavior and maxims for prudent political choice when it was revived almost 480 years later.

Consolidology

Consolidology, unlike transitology, has no such obvious a patron. It reflects a much more consistent preoccupation among students of politics with the conditions underlying *regime stability*. At least since Plato and Aristotle, theorists have sought to explain why—under the kaleidoscopic surface of events—stable patterns of authority and privilege manage to survive. While they have rarely devoted much explicit attention to the choices and processes that brought about such institutions in the first place—this would be, strictly speaking, the substantive domain of consolidology—they and their empirical acolytes have amassed veritable libraries on the subject of how polities succeed in reproducing themselves over extended periods of time. It does not seem (to me) excessive to claim that political science in the United States since World War II has been obsessed with the issue of "democratic stability" in the face of class conflict, ideological polarization, Communist aggression, North-South tensions, and so forth.

The consolidologist, therefore, has a lot of "orthodox" theoretical assumptions and "well-established" empirical material to draw upon. However, if the consolidologist has previously been practicing transitology, it will be necessary to make some major personal and professional adjustments. The consolidation of democracy (CoD) poses distinctive problems to political actors and, hence, to those who seek to understand (usually retrospectively) what these actors are doing. It is not just a prolongation of the transition from authoritarian rule. CoD engages different actors, behaviors, processes, values, and resources. This is not to say that everything changes when a polity "shifts" toward it. Many of the persons and collectivities will be the same, but they will be facing different problems, making different calculations, and (hopefully) behaving in different ways.

Tensions Between Transitology and Consolidology

This suggests possible contradictions between stages of the regime change process and the pseudosciences seeking to explain them. The "enabling conditions" that were most conducive to reducing and mastering the uncertainty of the transition may turn into "confining conditions" that can make consolidation more difficult. The shift in the substance of politics tends to reduce the significance of actors who previously played a central role and to enhance that of others who, by prudence or impotence, were marginal to the demise of autocracy or the earlier phases of transition.

The transitologist who becomes a consolidologist must make an epistemological shift in order to follow the behavioral changes that the actors themselves are undergoing. During the early stage of regime transformation, when an exaggerated form of "political causality" tends to predominate, the situation is one of rapid change, high risk, shifting interests, and indeterminate strategic reactions. Actors believe they are engaged in a "war of movement," in which dramatic options are available and the outcome, critically, depends on their choices. They find it difficult to specify beforehand which classes, sectors, institutions, or groups will support their efforts; indeed, most of these collectivities are likely to be divided or hesitant about what to do. Once this heady, dangerous moment has passed, some of the actors begin to "settle into the trenches." Hopefully, they will be compelled to organize their internal structures more predictably, consult their constituencies more regularly, mobilize their resource bases more reliably, and consider the long-term consequences of their actions more seriously. In so doing, they will inevitably experience the constraints imposed by deeply rooted material deficiencies and normative habits, most of which have not changed with the fall of the ancien régime.

The consolidologist must shift from thinking in terms of an exciting form of "political causality," in which unpredictable and often courageous individuals take singular and even unprecedented choices, and adjust to analyzing a much more settled form of "bounded rationality"—a form conditioned by capitalist class relations, long-standing cultural and ethnic cleavages, and persistent status conflicts and international antagonisms, and that is staffed by increasingly professional, predictable politicians. From the excitement and underdetermination of the transition from autocracy, the consolidologist must adjust to the increasingly prosaic routine and overdetermination of consolidated democracy.

The Pitfalls and Fallacies of Consolidology

The likelihood that practitioners of this embryonic subdiscipline can draw more confidently on previous scholarly work should be comforting. However, a great deal of work remains to be done before we understand how the behavior of actors can become more predictable, how the rules of democracy can be made more mutually acceptable, and how the interactions of power and influence can settle into more stable patterns.

Apprentice consolidologists in the contemporary world have two special problems:

1. They must sift through the experience of established liberal democracies (LDs) in order to separate the idiosyncratic and contingent properties from the eventual outcomes.
2. They must decide to what extent lessons taken from these past experiences can be applied to the present dilemmas of neodemocracies (NDs).

The fallacies of "retrospective determinism" (assuming that what did happen is what had to happen) and of "presentism" (assuming that the motives and perceptions of the past are the same as those of the present) are all too tempting. These fallacies can easily defeat the credibility of the consolidologist's efforts.[2]

But, to suspend incredulity for a moment, imagine a situation in which transitology and consolidology have become innovative and significant subdisciplines within the broader scope of political science. In the light of a book such as this and what has been written recently by others, what might be the fundamental assumptions of these two pseudosciences? What general maxims would be most useful in orienting future research and in guiding the practice of politicians?

In my current research on Southern and Eastern Europe and in my previous work on Latin America, I have collected and articulated a substantial number of fundamental assumptions, tentative maxims, and just plain working hypotheses about both transitology and consolidology. Most of those on transitology focus on the implications of *uncertainty* in rules, persons, and outcomes; highlight *unexpectedness* in the timing of events, processes, and cycles. They can be found in the book I wrote with Guillermo O'Donnell and I will not repeat them here.[3]

For the purposes of this volume, I have extracted and condensed nine "generic reflections" about consolidology. I leave it to the reader to determine whether, together, they constitute a promising foundation for this new pseudoscience.

> *First Reflection. Democracy is not inevitable and it is revocable. Democracy is not necessary: it does not fulfill a functional requisite for capitalism, nor does it respond to some ethical imperative of social evolution.*

Hence, its consolidation requires a continuous and extraordinary effort. Only after a lengthy period of "habituation" can politicians and citizens look forward to the routinized, and usually boring, perpetuation of stable democracy. Even then, there is always the prospect of a subsequent "deconsolidation" as institutions fail to adapt to changing external parameters.

> *Second Reflection. Transitions from autocratic or authoritarian regimes can lead to diverse outcomes.*

Four such transitions seem to be generically possible, although their probability varies considerably from case to case. The first is a regression to autocracy. Based solely on the historical experience of the three previous waves of democratization, this seems to be the most probable outcome. Few countries have reached democracy on their first try or by strictly linear and incremental means. Most had to revert to some version of the status quo ante or to pass through periods of rule by force. Some countries (e.g., Bolivia, Ecuador, Thailand, Turkey, and Nigeria) have oscillated between autocracy and democracy for protracted periods.

Nevertheless, each wave left in its wake instances of *consolidated* democracy. There are several reasons to suspect that the present wave may leave behind more such successful cases—both more of them and more widely distributed around the world—if only because so many of the countries involved have already tried and failed several times. But it is sobering to recall that in statistical, static terms, regression to some form of autocracy remains the most likely end product.

The second possible outcome is the formation of a hybrid regime that does not satisfy the minimal procedural criteria for political democracy but that does not regress to the status quo ante. O'Donnell and I attempted to define two of these hybrids. One (using a term invented in Spain during the 1920s to label the regime of Primo de Rivera) we called *dictablanda*. This is an authoritarian regime that liberalizes without democratizing; that is, it concedes certain rights and protections to people without permitting wide-spread participation in politics or subjecting its authority to popular accountability. For the other hybrid, we coined *democradura*. In these cases, the forms of democracy persist—especially, regular elections. But the opportunity for specific groups to participate—to propose candidates and to have their votes honestly and equally counted—is restricted, the constitutionally guaranteed liberal freedoms of expression and assembly are subject to interference by state authorities, and/or the capacity of elected representatives to act are limited by such nonelected and undemocratic officials as the armed forces, the police, or both.

The hybridization of democratic and autocratic elements probably does not constitute a stable and enduring solution to the generic problems of governance. It can, however, be a very useful improvisation in order to gain time, either for an eventual regression to autocracy (as seems increasingly to be the case in Africa) or for an eventual progression to some form of democracy (as seems to be the case in Guatemala and the Philippines, and as may become the case in Peru).

The third possible outcome may be the most insidious—and the most probable under contemporary circumstances. Rarely has it been identified by political theorists who prefer to work with more clearly defined and juxtaposed categories, and not to muddle about in "the excluded middle." This makes it especially difficult to identify and analyze what I propose to call *unconsolidated democracy*. Regimes trapped in this category are, in a sense, condemned to democracy without enjoying the consequences and advantages that it offers. They are stuck in a situation in which all the minimal procedural criteria for democracy are respected. Elections are held more or less frequently and more or less honestly. The various liberal freedoms exist—multiple political parties, independent interest associations, active social movements, and so on—but without mutually acceptable rules of the game to regulate the competition between the political forces. The actors do not manage to agree on the basic principles of cooperation and competition in the formation of governments and policies. Each party considers itself uniquely qualified to govern the country and does what it can to perpetuate itself in power. Each group acts only in the furtherance of its own immediate interests, without taking into consideration its impact upon the polity as a whole. Whatever formal rules have been enunciated (in the constitution or basic statutes) are treated as contingent arrangements to be bent or dismissed when the opportunity presents itself.

In discussions among political scientists, sociologists, and historians, this outcome has proven difficult to specify, even if there is considerable awareness that it may be the most likely fate awaiting contemporary NDs. One concept that has emerged, particularly in Eastern Europe, is that of *Argentinization*—so named because that country best exemplifies this dilemma, namely, repeated attempts at democratization that have not arrived at rules of fair play acceptable to all significant political and social actors and that collapse into authoritarian interludes. The fact that, in Argentina, in the past almost every elected government tried to manipulate the electoral law to its own advantage and that at present Menem has repealed the constitutional norm against presidential reelection to his own benefit offers clear evidence of the persistently unconsolidated status of the country's regime. Can it be a coincidence that people in Poland, the Czech Republic, Slovakia, and Romania have begun to talk about the prospective Argentinization of their NDs?

The fourth possible outcome is the most desirable one; namely, a democracy that is consolidated by mutually acceptable rules and valued institutions of fair play, tolerance, and competition. Defining the precise moment when this occurs, or measuring accurately the extent to which this has been accomplished, is not an easy task. Indeed, insisting upon it too much could lead to a contradiction in terms, because democracies are never completely consolidated. Democracies are unique in their presumed capability for self-transformation and in the degree to which they incorporate uncertainty into their normal functioning. Nevertheless, behind the changes in personnel, party, and policy that are intrinsic to this form of domination, namely, consolidated democracy, there are limits to the range of tolerable variation. These may be difficult to specify and measure in advance: some polities tolerate much greater "normal instability" than others.[4] But, when these limits have been exceeded, contingent consent breaks down and the process of deconsolidation becomes increasingly manifest.

Third Reflection. It is not democracy that is being consolidated, but one or another type of democracy.

There is no single kind of democracy; there are democracies. Many different rules and organizational forms can satisfy the criteria of contingent consent among politicians and gain the eventual assent of citizens. The central problem remains the same: how to come up with rules of competition and cooperation that the former will actively respect and the latter will passively (and belatedly) accept. But the possible solutions are varied. They are not, however, infinite, because they must ultimately respect the citizenship principle, if the polity is to become and remain democratic. At any given time, it is likely that some "foreign model" may appear to be preferable to all others, although efforts simply to imitate it will fail unless substantial modifications are made to accommodate national historical experiences, social and ethnic compositions, economic structures, international contexts, and so on.

> *Fourth Reflection. The type of democracy will depend significantly (but not exclusively) on the mode of transition from autocracy.*

My colleague and collaborator, Terry Karl, advanced the preceding hypothesis[5] in answer to the question: If so much diversity in rules and institutions are possible, what determines the selection of the type of democracy that actors will attempt to consolidate?

The very uncertain transition period sets the context within which actors choose the arrangements that are going to govern their future cooperation and competition. Most importantly, the mode of transition influences the identity and power relations of actors. Also, depending on the mode, they may be compelled to make choices in a great hurry, with imperfect information about the available alternatives and without much reflection about longer-term consequences. Their fleeting arrangements, temporary pacts, and improvised accommodations to crises tend to accumulate and to set precedents. Some may find their way into more formal, even constitutional, norms. It is, therefore, useful to consider the possibility of "birth defects" in the democratization process—defects due not only to structural features long present in the society but also to conjunctural circumstances that surround the moment of regime change. Each generic mode of transition seems to push toward a different outcome.

> *Fifth Reflection. Each type of democracy has a distinctive way of consolidating itself—especially as to own rhythm and sequence; no single path to consolidation is a guarantee for future stability or viability of all types of democracy.*

In other words, different types have distinctive problems and vulnerabilities. In the last instance, the success of CoD depends on social structures, the rates and extent of economic change, and cultural processes of political socialization and ethical evaluation—even though, at the time of transition, what counts are differences in the point of departure. These factors lie in the distant, unforeseeable future.

NDs in Latin America face an especially acute problem. In terms of status inequalities, income distribution, access to property, and economic marginalization, their initial situation is much worse than in the NDs of Europe, Asia, and Africa—and it is rapidly growing worse. So great are these disparities, that a number of well-informed observers (among them, Guillermo O'Donnell) have questioned whether it is conceivable that actors with such different resources will be able to come up with mutually acceptable rules.[6] Will they even be able to identify each other culturally as "fellow citizens," much less agree upon the defining line between the public and private realms, the appropriate scope for property rights, the mix of decision rules involving the counting of numbers and the weighing of intensities, and so forth? Past experience suggests not, but as noted earlier, there are sufficient new elements in the present equation— especially in the international context—that an eventually favorable outcome in Latin America cannot be ruled out.

The NDs of Eastern Europe and the former Soviet Union face the inverse challenge. Their points of departure are characterized by considerable equality in class, status, and income. The ineluctable coincidence of democratization with the transformation in that region from a planned economy to a market economy ensures that the first stages of regime change will be associated with radical increases in all forms of social, economic, and cultural inequality. This raises two questions:

1. Is it possible to consolidate some type of "Western-capitalist" democracy without the prior formation of stable and predictable cleavages based on class, sector, or profession?
2. Can this be accomplished while these cleavages are emerging in erratic and unpredictable ways?

Given the unprecedented nature of the situation, no one can answer either question with assurance.

Sixth Reflection. At this time in history, almost without exception democracy of one type or another is the only legitimate form of political domination.

Only some form of democracy can offer a stable consensual basis for the exercise of public authority. In the past, there were always alternative state regimes that seemed to be viable or that were perceived as more efficacious or desirable by certain social classes or groups. Today, the only competing supplier in the market at that level is the so-called Islamic state, and that, even in terms of potential, has only a restricted clientele.

But, as we have seen, this convergence in aspirations does not imply a convergence in trajectories and outcomes. The NDs of the fourth wave will attempt to adopt and adapt the current practices of LDs; hence, they will not follow (and, especially, they will not be able to repeat) the paths to democracy already trodden by the established democracies of Western Europe and North America. They will be invaded, whether they like it or not, by the most advanced institutions of present-day democracy, without having passed through the processes of gradualism, apprenticeship, and experimentation that were experienced by the older democracies. In other words, these latecomers are going to collect all the flora and fauna—including the most exotic species—of postmodern democracy—and almost all at the same time. This has relative advantages and disadvantages, but the main implication is that they will have to "catch up" in much less time and without being able to rely on preestablished strategies and rules.

This *unrepeatability* of the democratization process has incalculable consequences for the NDs, all connected with profound changes both in the domestic and international contexts and with the nature of the already established democracies. Unfortunately, most of these changes have been ignored by contemporary democratic theorists, which means it is very risky to extract valid lessons from the experience of the predecessors.[7] The embryonic sciences of transitology and consolidology are going to have to reflect on these ensuing changes. They cannot presume that the NDs of this present wave are going to repeat the patterns established by the previous three waves.

In the next four subsections, I outline four elements of unrepeatability.

Faster Rhythms

The rhythm of change in NDs will be much faster and compressed in time (but not in space where it has already been much more extensive). There will be much less time for hesitation, for allowing processes to mature, for making gradual concessions, or for being able to wait for a more propitious moment of economic growth or international circumstance.

Different Actors

The political actors will not be the same as before. The effective citizens of well-established democracies are organizations, not individuals.

These organizations are vastly better endowed, informed, and aware than were their forerunners. They can act in multiple sites, over a wider span of issues, and for more protracted periods. They can draw upon a greater variety of resources, domestic and foreign. Few NDs will begin with a full set of such "organizational citizens," but if and when their consolidation proceeds they will acquire them.

Analysts of the wave of democratization after World War II (particularly those studying the new nations of decolonized Africa and Asia) made the erroneous assumption that individual leaders, especially gifted, charismatic ones, would play the most significant role in guiding regime change to a successful conclusion. In countries where such leaders did emerge, they failed miserably—not just at democratization but at the creation of lasting institutions of governance. It is significant that the concept of charisma has almost never appeared in contemporary discourse about democratization and that the few experiments with highly personalistic leadership that have occurred (e.g., Alain García in Peru, Fernando Collor de Mello in Brazil, Lech Walesa in Poland) have not consolidated democratic institutions—in fact, quite the contrary.[8]

More Professionals

Most of the politicians who, through their respective organizations, participate in the process of regime change are not amateurs, but professionals. They may start out with little or no experience at the job, but they quickly learn to depend upon it. In short, politicians in modern democracies—both new and old—tend to live more and more *on* politics and less and less *for* politics. Frequently, they have no social status or economic base other than that provided by their elected or appointed position. They enter into politics with the intention of working at it full time and, if possible, for their entire professional life. This has profound implications for the formation of a distinctive political stratum and, particularly, for the way that the rotation of parties in power is organized—if in fact it is organized at all.

The New Diversity

Changes in domestic structures and international contexts have changed so much since the wave following World War II that contemporary democratizers cannot rely on the strategies of consolidation that were then relatively successful. There is so much more diversity in class, sectoral, and professional structures that the grand ideological formulas and partisan confrontations of the past are no longer convincing. Moreover, the end of the cold war and the collapse of Soviet power further contributed to fragmentation of symbolic identities and interest conceptions.

The tacit assumption that modern democracy would lead inexorably to "leftist" policies and an expansion of the role of the state, as competing parties offered public compensation and subsidization to broader constituencies, has given way to neoliberal expectations of the inverse: privatization, deregulation, monetary orthodoxy, balanced budgets, tax cuts, and the overriding importance of protecting property rights and the international competitiveness of producers. In my view, the "success" of neoliberalism could well be dispersed once its longer-term effects, especially on CoD, have been revealed and registered. But in the short to medium term it has meant that the NDs of Latin America, Eastern Europe, Asia, and Africa have emerged in an international ideological and programmatic context that is much more hostile to political solutions and capable of placing barriers in the way of institutional experimentation.

The Bottom Line

The four elements of unrepeatability just outlined lead to one conclusion: the role played by intermediary institutions—political parties, interest associations, and social movements—has changed irrevocably. All types of modern democracy are representative. Citizens, if they are able to hold rulers accountable, do so indirectly, that is, through the competition and cooperation of their representatives. Moreover, these channels of representation have developed, multiplied, specialized, professionalized, internationalized, and become increasingly autonomous. The NDs may not yet have acquired the full gamut of intermediaries—and the LDs themselves vary considerably in this regard—but they cannot avoid benefiting and suffering from these major changes.

The Declining Importance of Parties

To me, the most important of these changes is the decline in the historic role previously played by political parties. Their ideologies are no longer so convincing; their symbols are less present in everyday life; their patronage is less capable of providing welfare; their organizations cannot even replace the militants who die or desert their ranks; their leaders are less capable of mobilizing the public to attain collective goals—indeed, they are less and less successful in controlling the voting behavior of their members or even of inspiring them to vote at all. Parties now rarely provide individual citizens with their principal element of political self-identification and they are much less significant in the process of political socialization. They cannot demand the same discipline of their followers or even of their parliamentary deputies. They have lost their monopoly on the process of government formation—if they ever had it—and can no longer prevent other intermediaries from exercising influence over public policy.

Admittedly, the preceding résumé is exaggerated. Parties in LDs still vary a great deal in all these dimensions; moreover, their loss of functions may not prove to be irreversible. There is also no doubt, as Guillermo O'Donnell and I argued in *Transitions from Authoritarian Rule*, that parties in NDs emerge during transitions (although rarely do they promote or cause one) and come to play a dominant role in the structure of electoral competition and in the composition of early democratic governments. My hunch is that their role in the subsequent process of selecting and then consolidating institutions (i.e., in choosing the type of democracy) has been of less importance. In these domains, parties have had to share their power with other intermediaries, from state agencies to subnational governments, independent political personalities, and experts, not to mention interest associations and social movements. Even a king, Juan Carlos of Spain, seems to have had a major impact on the key decisions that lead to the selection and survival of these institutions. In several countries in South America, candidates have won presidential elections without the support of previously existing parties. In summary, one can say that political parties remain indispensable for the formal organization of electoral competition at all levels of government, but that they have lost a great deal in terms of militants, followers, internal participation, programmatic coherence, and credibility with the general public.

The Challenge of Social Movements

Neodemocracies have benefited and suffered from the coincidence that they emerged almost at the same time that "new social movements" were forming in LDs and penetrating their political processes. Some of these generic "causes" (e.g., feminism, pacifism, antiracism, regionalism, municipalism, environmentalism, and consumer protection) combined with demands that were more intrinsic to the problematic of regime change itself (human rights, political amnesty, compensation for victims, protection of ethnic minorities, civilian control over the military, institutionalized restraint over police behavior, and so on). The net effect has been to widen considerably the policy agenda. The tactics of protest of these movements, their extraparliamentary orientation, their mass mobilizations, and their concentration on single causes or themes diffused throughout the polity; in some cases, these factors made a major contribution to bringing down the ancien régime. Mostly, however, they contributed collectively—through the resurrection of civil society—to propelling timid and hesitant efforts at political liberalization into a more profound process of democratization.

The activity and importance of these social movements tend to diminish, however, once fair elections of uncertain outcome have been convoked and the first popularly elected government has been installed. This is, in large part, because some of their major demands have been met and they have trouble focusing on subsequent issues. It is my guess that, with few exceptions, such movements have not significantly altered the outcome; that is to say, they have not determined either the degree of consolidation or the type of democracy. Nevertheless, there is no doubt that their presence has broadened and complicated the policy agenda of most NDs.

The Role of Interest Associations

These brief reflections on the changing role of political parties and social movements leave us with the third generic category of intermediaries: associations that represent the specialized interests of classes, sectors, and professions. No one questions that the importance of these associations has increased in LDs or that NDs will have to confront and accommodate a wider range of better-organized interests than did their predecessors at a comparable stage of development.

To a degree, the rise in associability is responsible for the decline in the significance of political parties. The social classes that formed the historic bases for parties have fragmented into specialized sectoral and professional clienteles and have sought new forms of collective expression.

In the present wave of transitions in Southern Europe and Latin America, associations face specific problems. The system of interest intermediation that usually persisted in their previous authoritarian regimes was state corporatism, that is, one in which certain organizations were certified, if not created, by public authorities, guaranteed a monopoly of representation for specified categories, grouped into unique and preestablished national hierarchies, funded through public subsidies or obligatory contributions, and controlled either by a ministry or the ruling party. This type of corporatism was an artificial system, completely dependent upon the ancien régime and its continuous infusion of state coercion. During the present wave, in cases where there was no military defeat or foreign occupation (e.g., in Brazil, Argentina, Greece, and Turkey) it proved possible to conserve state corporatist institutions that were encrusted within an emergent system of multiple, competitive parties. Under the conditions of the fourth wave, this strategy of encrustation seems less viable, although the four countries just mentioned have been attempting (so far, successfully) to preserve important aspects of their past system of intermediation within their neodemocracies.[9]

But most contemporary NDs—not only in Southern Europe and Latin America but even more so in Eastern Europe—must face the difficult problem of dismantling their previous interest associations and replacing them with a new system of class, sectoral, and professional representation. Unlike Germany, Italy, and Japan, they are not going to be helped in this task by the direct intervention of foreign powers. The solution will have to come from within—from domestic political forces conditioned by party competition and the new freedoms of association, petition, and expression.

Pluralism and Corporatism as Alternatives

Two general alternatives are available, both of which are compatible with modern political democracy, even if they lead to quite different outcomes in terms of public policy, economic performance, and governability.[10] On the one hand, *pluralism* could emerge if the previous system degenerates into a set of autonomous, competitive, and overlapping organizations with strictly voluntary memberships and without any subsidization or control over their activities by the state. On the other hand, the former state corporatism could be replaced by *societal corporatism* if the previous system retains its basic structure of representational monopoly, official recognition, and hierarchic coordination, and if the new democratic government only indirectly supports existing associations through favorable financial and legal privileges and delegates to them major responsibilities for the making and implementing of public policies, but does not directly attempt to control their activities.

In those cases that I know best (Portugal and Spain), the transition initially produced a pluralist outcome, despite attempts to conserve the former corporatist institutions. It proved impossible to overcome two basic problems: (1) the weak legitimacy of organizations, imposed and artificially sustained over a lengthy period by the prior authoritarian regime as well as by their normative compatibility with the new political freedoms; (2) the incapacity of these organizations to adjust their financial structures from a basis of obligatory membership and contributions to one of voluntary contributions by voluntary members.

The consolidation of democracy in these countries brought about a major change, however. After a tumultuous period of high social conflict, sharp competition between rival ideological positions, and a great deal of experimentation in the delimitation of respective domains of interest, both systems evolved in the direction of societal corporatism. Periodic "social pacts" were made and there was regular incorporation of elite leadership and sectoral associations into policymaking at several levels. Based only on these two cases, I would conclude that there exists no direct and gradual path from state to societal corporatism. It seems that, with democratization, interest associations will have to pass through a stage of acute pluralism in which rival conceptions of the interests of classes, sectors, and professions will express themselves, measure their respective forces, and reestablish the legitimacy of this form of collective action. Only after this confrontation, and with some support from friendly governments and interested ministries, will the system of intermediaries evolve in the direction of societal corporatism.

The little that I have been able to learn about Asian transitions (specifically those of South Korea and Taiwan) seems to indicate that there, too, the immediate response has been a pluralization of previously state-controlled, monopolistic, hierarchical systems.

The NDs of Latin America display more variety. In Uruguay and Chile—the two countries with the strongest pluralist past and that in addition displayed relatively little effort to impose state corporatism during their authoritarian interludes—the transition, and now consolidation, has led rapidly to a new system of rather effective societal corporatism. This societal corporatism has accompanied the *pactismo* that has characterized the relations between civilians and the armed forces and between political parties. In contrast, in Brazil and Argentina—the two countries with an authentic tradition of state corporatism—the response has been more confused. In Argentina, Alfonsín attempted to impose pluralism by decree, and failed. The Argentine trade union movement has retained its previous structure, albeit with increased internal fragmentation and greater independence from the state. In Brazil, most of the legal dispositions of the former authoritarian regime have remained in vigor, including the obligatory "syndical tax" for workers, professionals, and capitalists. Nevertheless, rival competing organizations have emerged in some domains and all associations act with greater autonomy from state authorities.

> *Seventh Reflection. Transitions to democracy rarely happen in isolation—that is, without the simultaneous presence of other demands and other processes of profound change in socioeconomic structures and cultural values.*

The circumstances that lead to the demise of autocracies are varied, but they invariably involve crises and deficiencies in several institutions and spheres of society. It will be difficult to restrict the agenda of change only to political transformations—to changes only in the rules of the game, in the access of citizens to participation, and in the accountability of rulers. In favored, but rare, cases, the ancien régime may have already accomplished some of the necessary tasks; for example, it may have established national identity and boundaries, imposed civilian control over the military, increased the efficiency of the fiscal system, privatized inefficient state enterprises, or stabilized the value of national currency. Normally, however, the inverse is the case and neodemocrats inherit an accumulation of problems in various social, economic, and cultural domains, along with the inevitable problems of political structure and practice.

The Importance of Sequencing

The first implication of this unenviable situation is that the eventual outcome of democratization depends in large measure on the sequence with which the prime movers tackle the multiple transformations that are necessary. This, in turn, hinges on their collective capacity to control the political agenda sufficiently so that choices do not have to be made simultaneously. When the agenda becomes saturated and deals with various objectives at the same time, unwanted consequences and unusual combinations tend to emerge unexpectedly. For example, changes in the distribution of property might dislocate the system of production in the middle of an electoral campaign; local elections might coincide fortuitously with the implementation of a national policy on education or language use; the freeing of prices on products of primary necessity might happen before the stabilization of the exchange rate, or before the institutionalization of a system of collective bargaining; an attempt might be made to form a party system before the creation of a consensus on national identity and territorial limits.

Up to a point, these dysrhythmic and asyncronous happenings are normal. Even well-established LDs occasionally suffer from "unfortunate coincidences," despite the efforts of incumbent politicians to manipulate the political business cycle in their favor. The processes of economic, social, cultural, and political change have their own distinctive rhythms in terms of the time it takes to formulate issues, to mobilize their victors or victims, to decide on a course of action, to implement the policies chosen, and to register and absorb the effects of the policies. Democracies, especially presidential ones, impose upon themselves a rhythm fixed by the periodicity of the electoral cycle, which may or may not coincide with the trends, cycles, or events generated by other domains. In retrospect, it appears relatively easy to introduce some political reforms: to convoke elections, to revise the electoral rolls, to implement an electoral law, to recognize multiple parties, to concede civic freedoms, and so forth. Moreover, these reforms almost immediately affect both elite and mass behaviors, even if the results are not always what was predicted or is preferred. One of the reasons for this is that they combine or clash with other patterns of change that are slower, more diffuse, or less predictable. Any type of regime will have to face unexpected and unwanted coincidences, but the NDs are particularly susceptible to them simply because they are under pressure to accomplish so much in so little time and because the prime movers are more likely to lose control over the agenda of sequential responses.

What, then, is the optimal sequence for successful consolidation of democracy? If one could control the order of the day and manipulate it to avoid simultaneity—a utopian thought under present circumstances, especially in Eastern Europe and the former Soviet Republics—what should be done first? What second? What third? So far, economists have dominated the little overt discussion that has occurred. This has meant that:

1. Only such items as liberalization of prices, sale of public holdings, currency stabilization, deregulation, budgetary balance, elimination of industrial subsidies, and establishment of favorable incentives for foreign investment have been taken into consideration.
2. It has been widely presumed that these economic reforms should precede, not succeed, the consolidation of democracy.

Allegedly, unless one works fast to take advantage of initial enthusiasm and imposes "shock treatments" (large, comprehensive packages) before the affected groups and individuals can get organized to defend their changing, but nonetheless vested, interests, it will prove impossible to effect the reforms.[11] However initially popular and insulated are the governing elites, the fact that such actions virtually guarantee that it will be more difficult to consolidate democracy in the longer run does not seem to have been taken into account.[12] As apprentice consolidologists, it is our responsibility to inform those in power of the eventual political consequences of their choices, and to remind them that democracy (even liberal democracy) is not just an arrangement for protecting property rights and ensuring the most efficient operation of a capitalist economy.

Unfortunately, consolidology has a long way to go before it can provide a credible, "scientific" answer to this crucial issue of sequencing. Even if it can aspire to a higher degree of predictability than the meager 50 percent of transitology, and even if the number of cases in this fourth wave has already increased to the point that its practitioners can now bring the impressive apparatus of social statistics to bear on its subject matter, the pseudodiscipline is still in its inductive, if not intuitive, stage of development. It can hardly be expected to compete with the dazzling displays of economic scientists, even if the latter do occasionally admit to the unprecedented nature of the transformations they are called to comment and give advice upon.

Settling on a Territory

There is, however, one rule that all consolidologists are likely to agree upon: *It is preferable, if not indispensable, that national identity and territorial limits be established before introducing reforms in political (or economic) institutions.*[13] Moreover, there is no democratic way of deciding what should be the effective political unit. It cannot be settled, democratically, either by normal or exceptional means. Self-determination of peoples or nations is an appealing phrase, but it tells us nothing about how this determination is to be made. The classical mechanism, used frequently after World War I and occasionally after World War II, is the plebiscite. This, however, simply leaves in abeyance crucial questions as to who is eligible to participate and as to what is to be done about the rights of ensuing minorities.

It is a sad fact that modern, consolidated democracy depends on obscure and extremely complicated historical processes that were, themselves, not democratic. These acts of war, marriage negotiation, and empire somehow produced physical boundaries and cultural identities that have come to be accepted by their respective populations as appropriate, even natural. Within their so-called given confines, these populations agree to practice democracy.

The case of postauthoritarian Spain shows that it is possible for ethnolinguistic minorities to question these givens during regime transition without eliminating the possibility of a democratic outcome—but only when a prior minimal consensus on national institutions exists, and only when regional dissidents accept a deferred commitment to revision of the territorial division of authority. Without such continuity at the center and such trust in the periphery, the outcome might have been quite different. Moreover, one should not forget that a minority of Basque militants refused to accept this sequential and compromised formula, continuously challenging the neodemocracy and leaving many victims in the wake of the change. Only time will tell whether Turkey's decision to deal more intransigently with its Kurdish minority will not undermine its latest experiment with democracy.

With regard to this historic, so-called prerequisite, the countries of Latin America seem to be relatively favored. Despite considerable ethnic diversity and extremely high levels of income disparity, both personal and regional, national identities and boundaries do not seem to have been called into question by the explosion of demands that usually accompanies democratization. Indeed, in the case of the Southern Cone countries it can be argued that their forms of democracy allowed them to resolve boundary issues and to enter into a process of regional integration that would have been inconceivable under authoritarian regimes.[14]

It is in Eastern Europe and the successor republics of the former Soviet Union that "the national question" has taken on the greatest significance.[15] Acting in concert, the forces of liberation from imperial tutelage and of democratization have raised issues relating to both external boundaries (boundaries that do not correspond to national self-definitions) and to internal barriers (barriers to full citizenship and legal equality). Consolidologists have little to offer here —only a few, not very compelling suggestions about how to engineer party systems and to promote associations and territorial units that will maximize the opportunities for elite cooperation across ethnoreligious lines, then to reiterate the pessimistic message that it is difficult to imagine any progress being made toward CoD until the actors somehow agree upon a demarcation of their respective "national" units. Worse yet, consolidologists have to admit that there is no reliable democratic way to arrive at such a solution: only military victory, protracted stalemate, or mutual exhaustion, coupled eventually with diplomatic negotiation and treaty making, seem to have worked in the past.[16] Almost the only encouraging novelty on the horizon is that the "international community," as expressed through regional or global institutions, has shown willingness to intervene actively to bring about peace settlements in such conflicts and to provide scarce resources to those parties who agree to solve their disputes peacefully and democratically.[17]

Tortoises and Hares

Beyond such unoriginal and rather obvious observations about the early need for an acceptable political unit, I suspect that consolidologists will probably diverge—once they exist in sufficient numbers— in any further interpretations. My hunch is that they will form two schools. I will call the first, the Tortoises, the second, the Hares.

The Tortoises will draw their inspiration primarily from the country that has long been regarded as the classic democratizer, namely, the United Kingdom. Britain's case seems to prove that the process of consolidation is not only slow, taking centuries, not decades, it is also epiphenomenal. At Tortoise-pace, only after having gradually satisfied a vast number of prerequisites can a country expect to live comfortably with democratic laws and practices, unless that country is lucky enough to have inherited them from Britain itself. The optimal sequence is more or less clear: first, the formation of a nation-state; next, civilian control is established over the military, with diminution of arbitrary executive power and increased protection of private property, the creation of an entrepreneurial national bourgeoisie, the accumulation of capital, the attainment of a relatively high standard of living, and the indoctrination of the population into a "civic culture"—hopefully, before and not after it is gradually enfranchised and allowed freely to form associations. With slight modifications (especially in the timing of enfranchisement and freedom of association), this model can serve to explain the successful outcome of the US, Canadian, Australian, and New Zealand democratizations. With adjustments, it can be made to fit the gradualist pattern of the Nordic countries, the Netherlands, and Belgium, with the case of Switzerland requiring a bit more fine tuning.

The Hares are likely to look to the tortuous path that France took to democracy. France has periodically leaped over evolutionary stages during its repeated revolutionary episodes and experimented with a number of "prematurely" democratic reforms: republicanism, universal suffrage, a written constitution, a declaration of human rights, popular mobilization and direct mass participation, universal conscription, large-scale expropriation and distribution of land, emancipation from slavery, religious equality, and acceptance of political refugees. None of these worked particularly well the first time around, but they did eventually accumulate into the basis for a durable "republican synthesis." The literature tends to stress the much greater stability of the United Kingdom, especially in the eighteenth and nineteenth centuries; but this view overlooks the fact that the French—having voted for a republic in 1871 by a majority of one vote[18]—went on to retain democratic institutions until 1940, when they were defeated by the Nazis. During this period, France was more democratic than Britain, by virtually any standard. Since World War II and despite initial governmental (but not regime) instability, and a partial regime change in 1958, the French rate of socioeconomic transformation has far outstripped that of the British. France's current institutions are much more appealing to contemporary NDs than are those of its island neighbor.

Suspicions of a Hare

This brief comparison between Tortoises and Hares is only to show the *equifinality* of democratization. Different sequences of economic, social, cultural, and political change can lead to the same outcome, even to relatively similar types of democracy and patterns of public policy. Needless to say, this is a regrettable methodological inconvenience. No doubt it will plague the future scientific development of consolidology.

Much of the advice currently being fed to neodemocratizers, especially to those in Eastern Europe, seems to be coming from the (unknowing) Tortoises. They assign a clear priority to the development of capitalism and the formation of an individualistic "civic culture." They counsel an economics of massive and sudden innovation and a politics of gradualism. Explicitly, they stress the requirement that, domestically, leaders should be insulated from popular demands for immediate benefits and that they be protected in their economic orthodoxy by international political conditionality. Implicitly, the Tortoises seem to be arguing that democracy is a dispensable luxury for such under- or misdeveloped countries and that maybe it will take some "strong leadership" to get over the hurdles of accumulation.

As a (prospective) Hare, I am suspicious of this advice. Not only is the time frame of this wave too compressed to permit such political gradualism to work, but international norms more or less rule out the imposition of a *démocratie censitaire* or *capacitaire,* with its restricted franchise or limited social rights. In my view, it is likely that the level of economic development and the mix of public and private property are variables that can be manipulated, not constants that must be respected. And I am deeply convinced that the attainment of a civic culture is much more likely to come as a product of democracy than as a prerequisite for it.

Both the Tortoises and the Hares would certainly agree that the actors involved should, at all costs, try to avoid a situation in which economic and political transformations are made simultaneously, thereby confounding each other's outcomes in unforeseeable ways. To the extent that they can evaluate the respective rhythms and choose the timing of their interventions, those in governance should seek to manipulate and, if possible, separate their sequencing. This means that they should have a clear sense of reform priorities and be prepared to defend them publicly. The arena of disagreement is over which priority to uphold.

The Case for Putting Politics First

My Hare-ish assumption is that, to the extent that it is possible, political choices should be given priority over economic ones. Incentives for the restructuring of national political institutions should precede, temporally and functionally, those aimed at reforming national systems of production and distribution. In the consolidation of democracy, timing is a key element. For many of its choices, what happens or what is decided can be less important than when it happens or when it is decided.

This is not to argue that the transitional economy should be willfully neglected, especially given its dilapidated condition in most cases of regime change and the expectations of citizens concerning rapid improvement of their material well-being. But scarce resources must be devoted as soon as possible to such tasks as negotiating rules for electoral competition, convoking early and honest elections, stimulating the formation of a system of relatively disciplined parties, establishing collective bargaining between interest groups, consecrating an independent judiciary, organizing the legislative process, protecting freedoms of expression, association, and press, and, most importantly, drafting and ratifying a new constitution. If these political tasks are postponed, even for what appear to be good economic reasons, the momentum will be lost. It then becomes increasingly difficult to reach agreement on the rules of competition and cooperation that are basic to any type of democracy. It is desirable that those involved, the actors, take advantage of the uncertainty of outcomes and the indeterminacy of interests that surrounds the transitional period and move quickly to the choice of institutions that will consolidate a new regime.

Of course, these same arguments have been made by Tortoises in their defense of putting economics first. They stress that unless property rights, monetary stability, privatization of public enterprises, industrial restructuring, banking reform, sectoral deregulation, tariff liberalization, incentives for foreign investors, anti-inflationary policies, and so forth are rapidly put into place (and even simultaneously arrayed), the necessary measures will meet with increasing political resistance and, ultimately, fail to take hold.

In my view, this argument overlooks two key differences:

1. Economic policy choices are much easier to revise in future policy iterations than are political-institutional ones, either because the formal rules for amendment are much less restrictive or because it is easier to arrive at split-the-difference compromises over their content.
2. Market processes are much more insidious and invasive, because they tend to seek out and find equilibria, despite legal impediments and distorted incentives.

Making the wrong initial political-institutional choices (or neglecting to make them at all) sets in place more resilient practices that can be defended by the incumbent politicians that benefit from them. Vested economic interests will, of course, seek to do the same in favor of their protections, subsidies, and exemptions, but market forces (especially in a highly internationalized context) are more likely to undermine these efforts.

Eighth Reflection. Democracies tend to emerge "in waves."

There is a tendency for groups of democracies to occur during a relatively short time period and within a contiguous geographic area. Participants in the first cases of democratization (Portugal and Spain) could not have been conscious that their move would be instrumental in forming a wave that would eventually become almost worldwide. Each subsequent case, however, is linked to the ones previous, through processes of diffusion and imitation. Each success (or failure) creates a model, to be followed (or avoided).

The Increased Importance of the International Context

One major implication of the preceding reflection about waves of democratization is that the relevance of the international context tends to increase monotonically and to change in intensity with each successive demise of autocracy. The democracies that arrive late are destined to suffer more external influence than their predecessors. It would be risky to assume that these latecomers will learn from the mistakes of their predecessors, but it is possible to speculate that there are advantages to "delayed democratization," analogous to the economic advantages some economists claim for "late developers."

From this growing internationalization we can derive two consequences:

1. Each successive case of democratization contributes to the development of more formal organizations and informal networks for the promotion of human rights, the protection of ethnic minorities, the supervision of elections, the provision of political and economic advice, and the creation of interprofessional contacts. Since 1974, an entirely new infrastructure has been created at the international level for the promotion and protection of democracy. This infrastructure did not exist at the time of the first democratizations, in Southern Europe, when outsiders had to improvise to bring their influence to bear. Now, any country, anywhere in the world, even as it begins experimenting with democracy, is invaded by elements of the international environment—by movements, associations, party and private foundations, firms, and even individual personalities. The network of nongovernmental organizations has certainly contributed to the contemporary wave having, so far, produced few regressions to autocracy, at least in comparison with previous waves.

2. Moreover, the very existence of this embryonic "transnational civil society" seems to have influenced diplomatic behavior. Nations whose citizenries have most supported the efforts of the NGOs find themselves obligated at government level to support efforts at democratization in ways that go beyond normal calculations of "national interest."

Traditional protestations of "noninterference in domestic affairs" have become less compelling, and the line between the realms of national and international politics has become more blurred. Even more significant in the long run may be the increased reliance on multilateral diplomacy and international organizations to bring pressures to bear on the remaining autocracies or on recidivist democracies.

"Political conditionality" has taken a place alongside the "economic conditionality" practiced so long by the International Monetary Fund (IMF) and the International Bank for Reconstruction and Development (IBRD).[19] Global and regional organizations explicitly link the concession of credits, the negotiation of commercial agreements, the entry into the ranks of their memberships, and so forth to specific demands that the recipients take measures to reform political institutions, hold honest elections, respect human rights, and protect the physical safety and culture of ethnic or religious minorities. In extreme cases—and Eastern Europe seems to be one of them—the different levels of bilateral and multilateral conditionality combine in a way that considerably restricts the margin for maneuver available to new democratic leaders. Even more peculiar has been the spectacle of these leaders literally demanding to be subjected to international conditionality so that they can tell their people that they had no choice but to take certain unpopular decisions.

The European Community (EC), with its multiple levels and diverse incentives, has been of primary importance in the successful consolidation of democracy in Southern Europe.[20] The EC's role is also likely to be significant in Eastern Europe, despite the growing evidence of its members' unwillingness to make the same level of concessions and commitments in that area. The fiasco of the EC's inability to act collectively and decisively in preventing war between the former units of Yugoslavia is a sobering reminder of the limits of multilateralism.

No other region of the world has an institutional infrastructure as complex and resourceful as Western Europe's. In the Americas (through the Organization of American States) and in Africa (through the Organization of African Unity) some steps have been taken toward providing collective security for NDs and relaxing traditional inhibitions against interfering in the domestic affairs of members. The Arab League and the Association of Southeast Asian Nations have been conspicuously silent on the issue.

Even in Latin America, which has become almost saturated with international and institutional domination, pressures may mount on the few remaining autocracies. Recidivists may find themselves cast out of the fold. But neither pressure nor expulsion seems to be sufficient to guarantee democratization, as demonstrated by the cases of Cuba and Haiti.

Ninth Reflection. It is possible, but not necessarily easy, to move from various types of autocracy to various types of democracy without respecting the preconditions or prerequisites long considered to be indispensable by political science.

Based largely on the empirical cases of democratization in Southern Europe and South America, the embryonic science/art of consolidology has taught us that transitions of this magnitude can be made:

1. *without violence or the physical elimination of the protagonists of the previous autocracy.* Although most established liberal democracies did pass through a revolution or a civil war (or both, as was seen in the case of the United States) before achieving political stability, the NDs of the fourth wave have frequently managed to consolidate the new regime without such discontinuities or loss of life.

2. *without a great deal of popular mobilization that brings about the fall of the ancien régime and determines the timing of the transition.* Nevertheless, once the transition has begun (usually under other auspices), an explosion of mass participation often resurrects a dormant or suppressed civil society. This pushes the change process further than was intended by its initiators—and this in turn affects the pace and extent of eventual consolidation.

3. *without having attained a high level of economic development.* One could even affirm that democratization tends to bring about at least a momentary fall in the rate of economic growth—the price to be paid for freedom of assembly and expression, both of which revive long suppressed popular demands. In the longer term, however, these freedoms of action and thought are indispensable for sustained growth.

4. *without effecting a substantial redistribution of income or wealth.* Most citizens of neodemocracies seem not to harbor illusions about alternatives to capitalism based on radical equality. They have, therefore, proven surprisingly tolerant of existing inequalities—which is not to say that subsequent political competition will not aim at regulating capitalism's accumulative effort and better distributing its benefits.

5. *without the prior existence of a national bourgeoisie.* Not only has the existing bourgeoisie rarely been in the vanguard of the struggle for contemporary democracy, it has frequently been contaminated by its close association with the previous autocracy. With the emergence of highly mobile international capital, technology, and managerial skills, it is not as clear as it was in the past that development is contingent upon a dynamic group of native entrepreneurs.

6. *without a civic culture.* It has always been something of a mystery how individuals could expect to learn norms of mutual trust, tolerance, compromise, and personal efficacy under autocratic rule. But it is becoming increasingly obvious that democracy is compatible with a wide range of cultural dispositions—not just those that contributed to its emergence in the first place.

7. *without a large number of democrats.* Once politicians accept having to compete under specified rules, and prove willing to continue playing by these rules even when they have been defeated, and once citizens assent to these rules and come to accept the intrinsic uncertainty of the outcomes they produce, the minimal basis for democracy has been established. Only subsequently is one likely to find more convinced democrats behaving in a culturally civic fashion. What seems to count for more than a normative commitment to democracy, or more than a personal predilection to act democratically, is a pattern of group interactions that encourages contingent consent and reduces the boundaries of uncertainty.

No one—least of all a consolidologist—would question that some or all of the above conditions are desirable: nonviolence, popular mobilization, a high level of economic development, greater equality of income, a dynamic and liberal business class, a civic culture, and many democratically minded individuals. They may even be prerequisites for long-term stability—at least, they are likely to be produced by its regular functioning. That is not to say, however, that they are necessary (and they are certainly not sufficient) for the initiation and immediate consolidation of democracy.

The Coming Contest

I return to where I began. Democracy is not a necessity; it is a collective and contingent choice. It demands a continuous and extraordinary effort because it depends on a complex process of cooperation and competition that involves a large number of independent citizens—and because the formal equality it establishes in a limited political role is put in question every day by the informal equality of the socioeconomic system into which it is inserted.

The present wave of regime changes will crest and recede. I am convinced that it will leave behind more cases of consolidated democracy than all previous waves, and these democracies will be dispersed over a wider area. But some polities will be dragged by the undertow back to autocracy. The wave will produce a profound sense of *desencanto,* of disenchantment and disillusionment, when people discover that modern democracy does not resolve many of the palpable inequalities and unhappinesses of this world.

We are still far from "the end of history." To the contrary, I believe that once democracy has become the established norm within a region, and no longer has in front of it a rival type of regime—one markedly inferior—then, and only then, are the disenchanted citizens going to demand that their leaders explain why their persistent practices are so far removed from the ideals of democracy. I suspect that democracy consecrated will become democracy contested, and that the triumph of democracy in the last decade of this century will lead to a renewed criticism of democracy that will last well into the next century.

Notes

1. My debt to Machiavelli is made plain in the article I initially wrote on the subject of democratization: "Speculations about the Prospective Demise of Authoritarian Rule and Its Possible Consequences (I) & (II)," *Revista de Ciencia Política,* no. 1 (Lisbon, 1985), pp. 83–102 and no. 2 (1985), pp. 125–144. The quotation that follows is from Machiavelli, *The Prince,* VI. Peter Bondanella and Mark Musa, trans. *The Portable Machiavelli* (New York: Penguin, 1979).

2. The fallacy of retrospective determinism I learned from Reinhard Bendix, *Nation-Building & Citizenship* (New York: John Wiley, 1964), p. 13. The fallacy of presentism is discussed in David Hackett Fischer, *Historians' Fallacies* (New York: Harper Torchbooks, 1970), pp. 135–140.

3. Guillermo O'Donnell and Philippe C. Schmitter, *Transitions from Authoritarian Rule: Tentative Conclusions About Uncertain Democracies* (Baltimore, MD: Johns Hopkins University Press, 1986).

4. Nota bene: this implies that consolidation is not identical with stability. It is, therefore, quite possible for a democracy to be thoroughly consolidated and still quite unstable in such things as the composition of governments. Postwar Italy was an especially apposite case—until the recent deconsolidation of its long-standing arrangements for partisan distribution (*lottizazzione*).

5. Terry Lynn Karl, "Dilemmas of Democratization in Latin America," *Comparative Politics* 23 (October 1990), pp. 1–23. Also Terry Lynn Karl and Philippe C. Schmitter, "Modes of Transition in Southern and Eastern Europe, Southern and Central America," *International Social Science Journal* (May 1991), pp. 269–284.

6. Guillermo O'Donnell, "Delegative Democracy?" Working paper 173, Helen Kellogg Institute, University of Notre Dame (March 1992). Also O'Donnell "On the State: Democratization and Some Conceptual Problems: A Latin American View with Glances at Some Postcommunist Countries," *World Development* 21, no. 8 (August 1993), pp. 1355–1370.

7. An important exception is Robert A. Dahl, *Dilemmas of Pluralist Democracy* (New Haven: Yale University Press, 1982), where Dahl insists on the changing meanings and practices of democracy. Also Bernard Manin, "Métamorphoses du Gouvernement Représentatif," in Daniel Pécaud and Bernardo Sorj, eds., *Les Metamorphoses de la Représentation au Brésil et en Europe* (Paris: Editions du CNRS, 1991).

8. For a particularly strong (and, in my view, misplaced) emphasis on leadership, see Giuseppe Di Palma, *To Craft Democracies: An Essay on Democratic Transitions* (Berkeley: University of California Press, 1991).

9. See my "Organized Interests and Democratic Consolidation in Southern Europe," in N. Diamandorous, Richard Gunther, and Hans Jurgen Puhle, *Democratic Consolidation in Southern Europe* (Baltimore: Johns Hopkins University Press, 1995) where I make a detailed before-and-after comparison of the interest systems of Italy, Greece, Portugal, Spain, and Turkey.

10. See my "Interest Intermediation and Regime Governability in Advanced Industrial/Capitalist Polities," in S. Berger, ed., *Organizing Interests in Western Europe* (New York: Cambridge University Press, 1981), pp. 285–327 for evidence of the differential impact of these systems on elite instability, fiscal imbalance, and political violence during the 1960s and 1970s.

11. For an insightful, but supportive, treatment of the impact of economic shock treatments on political institutions in Eastern Europe, see Beverly Crawford, "Markets, States and Democracy: A Framework for Analysis of the Political Economy of Post-Communist Transformations," Working paper, Center for German and European Studies, University of California, Berkeley, 1993.

12. For a similar argument, see Adam Przeworski et al., *Sustainable Democracy* (New York: Cambridge University Press, 1995).

13. See Dankwart Rustow, "Transitions to Democracy: Toward a Dynamic Model," *Comparative Politics* 2, no. 3 (April 1970), pp. 337–363 for the original discussion of this "requisite."

14. I have explored this relationship in my "Change in Regime Type and Progress in International Relations," in E. Adler and B. Crawford, eds., *Progress in Postwar International Relations* (New York: Columbia University Press, 1991), pp. 89–127.

15. For an comprehensive survey, see Ian Bremmer and Ray Taras, eds., *Nations & Politics in the Soviet Successor States* (Cambridge: Cambridge University Press, 1993). For the argument that conditions particular to Eastern Europe and Communism are responsible for the especially salient role of nationalism in this area, see John A. Armstrong, "Toward a Framework for Considering Nationalism in Eastern Europe," *Eastern European Politics and Societies* 2, no. 2 (spring 1988), pp. 280–305. That is not to say democratization might not eventually prove to be subversive of existing national units in Africa, if and when the process becomes sufficiently rooted. The abortive elections in Nigeria showed that, despite a massive effort at "political engineering" by the authoritarian rulers, the voting patterns still followed closely regional and ethnic lines.

Inversely, the transition from autocracy in such Asian countries as the Philippines and Taiwan so far seem to have made it relatively easier to resolve (or, better, to defuse) long-standing conflicts along ethnic-cultural-religious cleavages. Malaysia has long run a *democradura* based on a delicate balance of "national" forces.

16. Even the "velvet divorce" of the Czech and Slovak republics was hardly a paradigm of democratic virtue. While the national elites involved were able to avoid violence, their solution was not subjected to a plebiscite by the citizenry of either country and seems to have depended on a rather momentary configuration of party strengths in the respective national assemblies.

17. For a case study of what may become a model for this multilateral intervention and coupling of peacemaking with democratization, see Terry Karl, "El Salvador's Negotiated Revolution," *Foreign Affairs* 7, no. 2 (spring 1992), pp. 147–164.

18. Adolphe Thiers, a monarchist, cast his deciding vote for the republic only because, as he put it, it is "the form of government that divides us the least."

19. I have explored the issue of conditionality in my "The International Context, Political Conditionality and the Consolidation of Neo-Democracies," paper presented at the SSRC Conference on International Dimensions of Liberalization and Democratization, Overseas Development Council, Washington DC, 15–16 April 1993.

20. See especially Geoffrey Pridham, "The Politics of the European Community, Transnational Networks and Democratic Transition in Southern Europe," in G. Pridham, ed., *Encouraging Democracy: The International Context of Regime Change in Southern Europe* (Leicester: Leicester University Press, 1991), pp. 212–245.

PART 2

DIFFICULTIES IN THE DEMOCRATIC PROCESS

2

Democracy and the Metaphor of Good Government

Edelberto Torres Rivas

The wealth of theoretical material dealing with democracy over the past ten years covers two basic aspects of what is presently taking place in Latin America. One, concerning transition, deals with the decline and collapse of authoritarian or military regimes. The other, concerning consolidation, debates the strategy that democratic forces need in order to encourage political institutions and a political culture and to boost public participation in them.

Democratic governments have been restored throughout Latin America. They are democratic because they are the result of contested, multiparty elections that grew out of a first flush of freedom. Tradition, political culture, the energy of the participants, and other local conditions by and large justify the epithet *democratic*. Efforts are being made to establish democratic regimes in Latin America. We may assume, then, that the permanence of democratic governments will eventually give way to democratic regimes.[1]

Let us remember that these days conservative thinkers use certain superficial aspects of political life as a means to power. By constant repetition of the word *election*, they have equated this tool of democracy with democracy itself. The terms *election* and *democracy* are not synonymous in the past or present experience of any Latin American country, and the false notion is best dispensed with. Elections, of course, hold a more than symbolic value in popular perception. In some instances, representing a return to practices suspended during authoritarian periods, elections uphold democratic tradition. More often, they mark the beginning of the citizen participation that goes

Edelberto Torres Rivas is former director of FLACSO, Costa Rica, and senior researcher, FLACSO, Ecuador.

DIFFICULTIES IN THE DEMOCRATIC PROCESS

hand in hand with the weakening, the decline, and the collapse of military dictatorships.

The value of an election, therefore, lies not in the fact itself but in the resulting democracy. Serious weaknesses have begun to emerge in recently elected civilian governments. These weaknesses appear against a backdrop of acute economic problems, political instability, and the still fresh scars of brutal human rights violations. After an election, people expect Good Government.

The Metaphor

In a brilliant essay dating from 1827, Charles Dupin, the French polytechnician who first used statistics in political economy, showed that two-thirds of the French people of the day had been born after the 1789 Revolution. This generation wanted a different country, a kindly society, and good government.[2] As a metaphor, the term *Good Government* suggests a desire for community mobilization. The reverse—bad government—may be more frequently heard as a popular grievance. Good Government, in fact, is an antimetaphor, for it takes the true meaning, the basic aspiration of all governments, to a figurative dimension that presumably does not exist—the quality of goodness. The term operates, really, as a symbolic summoning up of possibilities and expectations. Good Government is hopeful, elliptical. It is a metaphor for the democratic search to put public order in the service of addressing the problems of the majority.

Metaphor, which puts a figurative meaning onto the literal, in this instance is not tacit—as in literature—but forced. We depart from actual experience and appeal to rhetoric in order to make our analysis. A metaphor can guide our thoughts and bring our discussion to a scientific level.[3]

The poor performance of democratic governments in recent years has in difficult times made us think about the concept of Good Government. We should remember that, throughout history, man has fallen back on similar metaphors. The collapse of Athens caused Plato to imagine the Just State; in the military repression that began in 1976, Argentines spoke of a sick society.

Political Democracy and Good Government

We must not confuse the idea of "good government" with the concept of "democratic government," and even less with "political democracy," which has become an expression of democratic government.

For the reasons given below, we cannot always assume that good government will necessarily come out of a political democracy. Put another way, the existence of a political democracy does not guarantee good government, but good government, in the present context of Latin America, is only viable within a political democracy. A legitimately elected government is a positive step toward a postauthoritarian period and seeking a balance between the renewing forces of democracy and the outdated ones of authoritarianism. But more is needed to help consolidate democratic and electoral government. In viewing the historic developments taking place in Latin America today, it is important to make a distinction between the two processes.

Political democracy is that democracy that comes about through, and respects, the established rules of the game for determining candidates and how they will be chosen to make decisions affecting community life. Such democracy not only upholds the letter of the law but is the crowning glory of formal law. A political democracy constitutionally proclaims civil rights, public liberties, and so on, enshrining them in written texts. But good government seeks a permanent link between political freedom and social justice. Without social justice, there cannot be good government.

Political democracy, once it satisfies the rules, is the careful exercise of the right to vote. But in societies in crisis, good government also concerns itself with how decisions are put into practice and, above all, for whose benefit. The practice of good government can transform political democracy into social democracy. While there is no reason for not stating things this way, there are many for doing so.

In Latin America, inadequacies have not stemmed from electoral democracy itself but from the conditions in which it is currently emerging, and frequently from the consequences to which they have led. To be more specific, failings arise from the weaknesses of civilian governments elected under politically adverse conditions (the participation of political parties or other actors from a period of military dictatorship) or from economic difficulties (inflation, stagnation, and trade and fiscal deficits) or from grave social deprivation, such as that taking place at present.

It must be made clear, however, that in employing the metaphor "good government" I refer to the policies, procedures, and decisions addressing the problems that stem from a legacy of authoritarianism or from international economic crises. Such problems existed before recent democratic elections. It is important to *monitor* new politicians for the qualities they should (or should not) possess before they begin a public career in which they will have to tackle these problems. The argument I am trying to develop here—based on the experience of a great many civilian governments in the past few years—

is that, although there are problems that existed before the new administrations, and that are external to them, there are also internal perceptions, abilities, and wills inherent in the new democratic governments.

It is how problems are addressed that separates new governments from the incompetence of authoritarian or military governments. Many of the new governments are riddled with incompetence, impulsiveness, privilege, irresponsibility, and other vices that are far removed from the essence of Good Government. Policies for creating stability and change, for example, can be applied in many ways, orthodox or unorthodox, either for the benefit of a few or with the intention of protecting the impoverished majority.

What has happened to the democratic governments elected in many Latin American countries? Why since coming to power have they headed inevitably for self-doubt and self-destruction? Why are democratic civilian governments failing? It is these concerns that link the subject of democracy to that of good government. I want to consider the good government metaphor in the context of the shortcomings of civilian power presently to be found in public administration, such as the outrageous collapse of the first directly elected, democratic Brazilian government—that is, elected with high hopes for democracy. In Fernando Collor de Mello we have an appalling example of corruption in which it is hard to say which was worse: the extent of the looting or the speed with which it took place. Societies and the potential for real democracy have been damaged by the failure of civilian governments in Guatemala and El Salvador; the legal, moral, and political subterfuges of Alain García's administration and the *autogolpe* of Alberto Fujimori in Perú; and the decline of the public image and capacity of the last two presidents of Venezuela. Are the societies of Venezuela and Brazil intrinsically ungovernable, or do they suffer from lack of direction, outworn leadership, and rash disregard of the public good? And, finally, what can be said about the criminal collaboration between the military chiefs of civilian governments and drug lords in places like Colombia, Honduras, and Bolivia? The list of these examples of misconduct could go on endlessly.

New Aspects of Legitimacy

The legitimacy of public authority is inseparable from the interests of the community. The problem at present in Latin America is how to win over the loyalty of the masses when programs that impoverish the majority of citizens are implemented alongside expanded opportunities for democratic participation.

In today's context, it is no longer enough to cite historical examples or to echo Max Weber's idea of the rationality of law. Legitimacy nowadays is upheld by a broad faith in a mandate, a concept of obedience that the citizen or individual absorbs and that leads to stable public institutions. Obviously, a balanced relationship between command and obedience depends on the ability to cultivate a widespread belief that the system is legitimate. Why is it legitimate? As Latin America has recently come out of illegal and profoundly illegitimate military and authoritarian governments, it is presumed that elections are what make civilian governments legal. In fact, only good government can give them legitimacy. In other words, there is a new source of legitimacy, the demand by a majority that its basic needs be heeded and satisfied.

Let us remember that not every politically democratic struggle leads to democratic government, much less to a democratic regime. Political activity is sometimes reduced to a power struggle over control of the state apparatus. This results in irresponsible government. Good government does not mean ideal government but refers to the classical idea, stemming from Aristotle, that at the heart of any given political community the best administrators are those who concern themselves with community affairs. Concern with wise, appropriate, efficient management of public affairs looms even larger in Jean-Jacques Rousseau and in the critics of absolute monarchy. It is a consistent theme in mainstream political science.

It was also the overriding concern of that master of realpolitik, Niccolo Machiavelli, who, in his *Discourses on the First Ten Books of Titus Livy* (rather than in *The Prince*), put forward the idea that a prince should confer benefits on the populace. Only political adventurers, not wise princes, would look on evil and intolerable violence as necessary. Of course, he also counseled a prince to seek the approval of the people (*principato civile*), but on the grounds that they were manipulable. No one else since Aristotle has spoken so convincingly of the advantages of consensual politics or of agreement on taxation policy. Both found that satisfying people's needs, protecting their property, and eliminating dangerous inequalities were the keys to consensus.

In other words, in order to gain the loyalty of the people a government must address their problems. This process has less to do with a political democracy's constitution—the legality of its mandate

is enough—than it has with the quality of a government's administration, which alone can generate legitimacy. A society is more gov-
ernable when some form of social consensus is sought and built and
stability results from an effective channeling of social conflicts. A legitimate government is always a more stable government. What is immediately required is adding to the legality of the establishment of
the government the legitimacy of that government's later public action. Hence the need for good government, which is self-defining.

Many Latin American countries do not—and may not for some
time—have a democratic regime, and still less a democratic society.
Certain steps have been taken. More than ninety elections, at all levels, have occurred since the early 1980s. They have involved a widespread call for elections by disaffected citizens, who—if we are to
judge by the list of parties and candidates rather than by the variety
of their ideologies or their programs—have taken part in reasonably
contested elections. Moreover, these elections have with good reason
been labeled democratic, because there have been few allegations of
fraud in the returns—election fraud being the former, oligarchic way
in Latin America of choosing who should govern.

Another aspect of legitimacy is the Rule of Law, which can be variously defined. Legal theory has an extensive bibliography on the
subject of the state as a lofty legal organization arranged according
to principles and techniques that tend to limit the power of the governor. The principle of legality involves the submission of all public
administration to a preexisting judicial order.[4] Other elements of the
Rule of Law are: (1) that there exist a body of laws known in advance, (2) that these laws be observed, (3) that mechanisms are in
place to assure the observance of laws, (4) that provision is made for
conflicts to be resolved by an independent judiciary or by arbitrators,
and (5) that there are procedures to change laws when they no
longer do what they were intended to.

In the present circumstances, a new principle of legitimacy is required that will once again assure the loyalty of the masses without
leading to the volatile majorities that have occurred in recent elections. Consistency is needed, derived not from electoral chance or
political contingencies but from a stable participation by citizens and
by a government that will give as much commitment to social problems as to policies for economic growth. Claus Offe rightly wonders
whether state policies can effectively legitimize sociopolitical institutions in a capitalist state.[5] During economic crises, social reform flags
and, even more rapidly, the bases of consensus grow weak. This is the
cause behind the crisis of legitimacy that may threaten electoral
democracies.

The Problem of Efficiency

For a transition from an electoral democracy to a democratic society to occur—however we define the latter—a great stretch of road must be traveled toward efficient public administration, a new state rationality, new skills, and a strategy for government. Achieving these elements is the best way to serve the community and legitimize the rule of democratic governments. Legitimacy is dependent on efficiency, which can be defined as a historic rationale for producing certain goals pertaining to the common good.

At present, in a period of change in productive and political structures and of uncertainties in social development, good government must be efficient government. A number of international forums have called for a new "institutional capacity" that will help the public sector take on its duties responsibly. To achieve this, human resources of an appropriate technical caliber must be found; otherwise arbitrariness and incompetence will continue raising havoc with community resources, plans for change, and the trust placed in the new democracies.

Democratic governments must base their efficiency from the outset on basic, formal mechanisms that will prevent random enforcement of laws; that will take constant care not to violate constitutional norms; that will always show absolute clarity in the management of financial resources; that will responsibly use discretionary powers that affect large parts of the population; that will take care not to squander resources; that will steer clear of privilege and influence peddling, and so forth. The efficiency expected of good government, or the internal management that defines it, is guaranteed in North American and European countries by public accountability, which is regulated, open, and respected.[6]

It should not be a matter for surprise that the question of efficiency is so closely linked with the consolidation of democratic governments. But at the present time—when elections are demanded in a context of scarce resources—it is more than ever necessary to have governments that will deal with society's most urgent problems with some degree of efficiency. Efficiency is the ability to carry out election promises; or, more broadly, it is the ability to achieve established targets. In a postliberal atmosphere like the current one, these are not targets determined by the market but by society at large.

What I am trying to point out here is the need to endow recent democratic governments with a new logic in their decision-making processes so that they will have a bias toward problems that I shall describe as general, national, and global, as an antonym for private, class, or corporate interests. Efficiency, then, must go hand in hand with, or be the permanent expression of, a political will to deal with—not necessarily to resolve—the community's most pressing problems.

The relative failure of civilian governments is clearly owed to inefficiency in the running of state industries by opportunistic politicians, new officials, possibly devoted social activists, and others whom electoral democracy promotes simply in order to renew bureaucratic personnel for a new period. This is often so because party loyalty is more highly valued than technical skills. At other times, tension arises between hopes placed on electoral pledges and the frustration generated by cynical disregard for their fulfillment. Secondary, irrelevant policies may be brought in that have nothing to do with election promises. In some countries (in Central America, for example) decline clearly stems from a complete inability to end political violence and uphold human rights.

Such modest aspirations, such a bare minimum of goals and skills, makes sense only in Central America, where hopes for security, peace, and prosperity have been set back by war and other violence for half a decade or more. What is clear is that the violence and war, a result of age-old injustice, has further increased the aspiration. Of the 250,000 dead, 85 percent are noncombatant civilians. In Guatemala, El Salvador, and Nicaragua, average real incomes declined by 18 to 25 percent over ten years. Forty percent of the population, although unaware of the statistics, dropped below poverty to underclass status. Civil war, when it is an armed social conflict, is the worst kind of war, and its consequences for a return to normality are appalling. It brings to a standstill all work, building, study, production, and pleasure.

This is why, when thinking about good government, we have to take into account what making life normal again in Central America entails (in other countries, good government can be brought about in other ways). This has to do with campaigns that result in the haphazard election of personalities on the fringes of political life—people who know nothing about public affairs or community needs. Charisma is haphazard, and administrative ability is not required for success in elections. Electoral democracy does not guarantee that candidates of good quality will be chosen. It is a matter of concern that nowadays electioneering can be manipulated by newcomers who command great financial resources or who control media empires or whose credentials amount to a name or some other inherited attribute. In Latin America we have had extreme cases of figures catapulted out of show business—singers with good voices, personalities with good looks or money, television celebrities, or people who emerge from apolitical backgrounds against the grain of deep social challenges.

It is important to define the criteria by which efficiency is determined. Both administrative and ethical factors must be considered. Efficiency must be judged according to how a government addresses the grave social problems without whose resolution there will be no stability, governability, or democracy.

Morality and Public Life

Ethical criteria now seem to be more crucial than ever. To apply morality to public life is often the last but not the least important task of good government.[7] Recent experience in various countries seems to confirm that socioeconomic crises do not favor the emergence of morally responsible leaders. Those who enter politics as a vocation do not always fit Weber's definition of the statesman as a man who rises above his immediate fortunes and, beyond his surroundings, sees horizons that confirm his steadfastness, that enable him to set himself above personal appetites and party ties, and to concentrate on the higher values of solidarity, the common good, and human dignity. In similar vein, Victoria Camp writes: "The public virtues that I am thinking about do not depart from a new community relationship but try to compensate for the lack of community; they depart from imperfect democratic reality—that is, from the requirement of dialogue for making decisions about collective problems, the first of which and the condition of the democratic procedure itself is to succeed in gaining individual dignity for each member of society."[8]

Can we today talk meaningfully about morality? Public morality, that is, because private vices are difficult to assess in the present, predominantly postliberal, climate. The Greeks, Aristotle, thought that virtue (*arete*) was second nature to man; that it was the quality that allowed him to fulfill his destiny. Politics is virtuous to the extent to which it perfectly carries out its function. But in modern ethics, the focus has changed from virtue to duty.[9] And in our present-day, wild glorification of private and corporate interests stimulated by market values, the question we should ask is: Duty to whom? The answer is public duty, the morality of community life.

Morality cannot be only private, since "the scope of morality, where it is possible and necessary to regulate and judge, is that of actions and decisions that have repercussion in the community or that are of common interest."[10] There is an urgent need to inject morality into public life and politics and to restore the notion that successful work is that which benefits the majority. The characteristics of such work are solidarity, responsibility, and tolerance. In politics, the virtuous individual is the public figure, just as in the marketplace the successful person is the executive. The good politician is not the one who only wins elections but the one who carries out good government.

In certain Central American countries, a political strategy based on respect for human rights is the only defensible point of departure—the kickstart of good government administration. This strategy has two aspects. One is to guarantee human rights; the other is to ensure the punishment of those responsible for human rights violations. To uphold the rule of law, to respect legality, is to bring about the demise of impunity. For example, a strong, independent judiciary, without military jurisdiction or amnesties for the armed forces, is required; as is constitutional government in which constitutional norms are absolute and enforced.

A recurrent problem that threatens public morality today is public corruption. The evil of easy money is more corrosive now than ever, because personal success has to be exhibited in the form of luxury, ostentation, and consumer prosperity. The politician, the bureaucrat, the successful government official must show these things publicly; otherwise, they are thought not to be successful. Contagious venality—becoming corrupt and corrupting others—in public management of the community is damaging the building of democracy in Latin America as never before. Political corruption is not in itself a new phenomenon, but in its current pathological dimension (with inefficiency, authoritarianism, drug trafficking, and so on) private business and public interest have become confused. The latter has let itself be infiltrated by the morality of the marketplace. Corruption is the arbitrary decision that benefits the person who buys favors, which is another way of confusing public with private interest. Corruption undermines the citizen's confidence; it demoralizes and bewilders. Good Government requires an undamaged public morality.

Political corruption has another aspect. The conduct of a politician who misbehaves in private life becomes a public matter, the province of the media. However, the public does not have to resort to pettiness and hypocrisy. This is not to say that private vices are acceptable, because scandal in private life can taint political life and responsibility.

The Necessary Minimum

In conclusion, it must be repeated that the elements and conditions that make up good government should not depend exclusively on the will of those at the top. Good government should not be an aim only of those who govern: it should be an ongoing demand by those who are governed. Initiatives, pressures, and various forms of participation must derive from society at large.[11] The action taken by its members should be collective rather than individual. Society at large should organize, make demands, debate, create public opinion, and bring pressure to bear. Civic life is strengthened when policy is made by individuals influencing the public sphere. A citizen is only a citizen through participation in political decisionmaking. The state must guarantee the citizen the chance so to participate; in the end, this chance becomes the exercising of a right.

Good government is good only when it can accept and assimilate new and old expressions of social nonconformism. Without struggle and conflict, civic society decays. Good government accepts nonconformism, mitigating its presence and its effects. Nonconformism is also shaped by public opinion, which in part dictates its dynamic. Political parties, social organizations, and the world of nongovernmental organizations can be outlets for this process. Plans for change should come not only from government but be generated by the people. Without prospects of change, a society is not a fully fledged society. Good Government accepts, promotes, receives, and acts on such plans. It bears pointing out that under a dictatorship there is no public opinion. The creation of public opinion is the essence of civil society, and in a dictatorship, public opinion becomes fragmented, passive, and unbalanced.[12]

The metaphor of good government can be understood as a strategy necessary to avoid discrediting the electoral system, the democratic premise, civilian governments chosen for their promises and programs, or politics itself. Above all, the metaphor is necessary to avoid damaging the credibility of public life. Good government restores the social basis of community life, which violence and economic crises have so profoundly altered.[13]

What is essential is that people have at least a minimum of confidence in political institutions, and in plans for change. They must have confidence that whatever the present difficulties, the future will be better. A generation must come that will find that its rights are respected, that in another five years will be able to say that, bad as things may still be, they are better than they were. Herein lies the present political, ethical, and cultural virtue of the metaphor of good government.

Notes

This chapter was translated by Norman Thomas di Giovanni and Susan Ashe.

1. I use the terms *government* and *regime* to distinguish between the result of a democratic election and the product of a sustained historical democratic process. It is a makeshift distinction. At present there is a good deal of confusion over these concepts. I wish to employ the distinction in order to avoid becoming enmeshed in the old, unresolved polemic between "real" and "formal" democracy, or in the even more problematic debate between "social" and "political" democracy. The persistent need for such distinctions, however, points to real problems that have no solution.

2. Andrä Tudesq, "La France Romantique et Bourgeoise, 1815–1848," in G. Duby, *Histoire de la France* (Paris: Editorial Larousse, 1956), p. 381.

3. Francisco Delich, "La metáfora de la sociedad enferma," in *Crítica y Utopía* nos. 10 and 11, Nov., Buenos Aires, 1983, p. 14. Delich clearly illustrates the use of metaphor in the social sciences in his analysis of Argentinian society during the military regime. As with a living organism, a society at odds with itself is a sick society.

4. David Ruccio, "When failure becomes success: Class and the debate over stabilization and adjustment," Kellogg Institute, Notre Dame University, April, 1989, mimeographed paper. Ruccio analyzes various experiences in which policies of stabilization and change, considered to be failures owing to the poverty to which they have given rise, should really be looked on as successes, owing to the wealth they have brought to powerful groups.

5. Claus Offe, *Contradicciones en el estado de bienestar* (Madrid: Alianza Editorial, 1990), especially Chapter 3.

6. Good Government may be confused with Public Management. The two terms can be used interchangeably, but management is closer to public administration of private business, government to public management of community business. It is a matter of emphasis.

7. Social scientists are prone to making seemingly obvious statements such as this one about morality. They are the professionals who analyze and think about social behavior—but they are themselves social animals. The problem is an inevitable one. The obvious must, however, be stated.

8. Quoted from Camps's authoritative *Virtudes públicas* (Madrid: Espasa-Manaña, 1990), p. 24.

9. Alastair MacIntyre, *Tras la virtud* (Barcelona: Editorial Crítica, 1988), Chapter 2.

10. Camps, *Virtudes*, p. 116.

11. I have dealt with this subject in my essay "Sociedad civil y participación política," presented at the Encuentro Iberoamericano de ONGs, Cuenca, 8–10 July, 1992.

12. Democracy today should be founded on the creation of new public spheres not necessarily state-sponsored and on new private spheres are not linked to the marketplace. Cf. John Keane, *Public Life and Late Capitalism:*

Toward a Socialist Theory of Democracy (New York: Cambridge University Press, 1984).

13. In Central America, this does not only imply having confidence in the government in the abstract; it means no longer having to fear the policeman on his beat.

3

Democracy and the Limits of Popular Sovereignty in South America

Susan Stokes

The early literature on redemocratization in Latin America was openly celebratory: alongside the causal analyses and clear-eyed prognoses was a warm embrace, and more than a touch of euphoria.[1] So self-evident was the superiority of democratic over authoritarian regimes to writers and readers alike that it was unnecessary to lay out the reasons why. The most influential work on the transition simply affirmed that "political democracy constitutes per se a desirable goal."[2]

As Latin America's democratic regimes grew out of early infancy, a more sober literature followed, much of it authored by Latin Americans.[3] Although no one seriously challenged the notion that even the most deficient democracies were preferable to military authoritarian regimes, the many deficiencies of the new democratic regimes were enumerated. They were found incapable of rooting out socioeconomic inequalities or of dealing adequately with economic crises. They were found timid in bringing to justice violators of human rights from the past period of military rule and sometimes generated their own human rights atrocities. Social movements that were broadly participatory helped bring the new democracies to power only to be squashed or dispersed once the normal politics of civilian rule was under way. And, in a nasty, brutish, and short kind of argument, the new democracies were unstable.

This chapter belongs to this second, more sober wave of works. I begin by making explicit one of the grounds for declaring democratic regimes superior to military authoritarian ones that implicitly

Susan Stokes is professor of political science at the University of Chicago.

motivated the first wave of works on regime transition: in democracy the people are sovereign, whereas in military authoritarian regimes they are not. Popular sovereignty in modern nation-states relies on representation, which in turn relies on accountability. The popular election of governments is thought to be the critical institutional pillar supporting accountability, representation, and rule of the demos. But in the second section, I draw attention to the recent record of elections and policymaking in several South American democracies to show that if elections have translated the popular will into policy they have done so in a manner that is anything but straightforward. In the third section, I outline some explanations for why these elections have failed to serve a function they would serve in a system of popular sovereignty. I conclude by indicating further lines of research that will enable us to understand how institutions of electoral democracies strengthen or weaken the link between elections and popular sovereignty.

Popular Sovereignty, Representation, and Accountability

We invoke the word *democracy* when speaking of modern republican governments because we consider them to be governments that act in pursuit of the people's interests, even though the people do not rule directly. The seventeenth-century invention of representative institutions grafted a version of democracy onto large-scale, highly complex nation-states. Representation, the making present of one who is absent, allowed the interests and preferences of the demos, though literally absent, to be made present in collective decisionmaking. Granted, many architects of republican institutions believed these institutions were more than just a pragmatic adjustment of democracy to the reality of large-scale, complex societies. They were an improvement on democracy by assembly (or any conceivable modern variant) because representatives would resist the "temporary errors and delusions" of the people, and would have time to make government a "special profession."[4] But most theorists of representative government agreed that popular election of representatives was required if government was to pursue the people's interests. Few believed, with Edmund Burke, that representation could be achieved without election.[5]

Elections were always, moreover, considered of necessity to be repeated at fixed intervals. Popular sovereignty could not be guaranteed by leaders elected once for indefinite terms. Life (or very long) tenure was preserved for special offices that were to be insulated from popular opinion. The architects of republican institutions generally assumed that representatives who did not face a future election would be susceptible to influence by powerful minorities, or to venality, or would be tempted to economize their effort, or for some other reason would deviate from the pursuit of the interests of the demos. Thus, representation rests on electoral accountability just as firmly as popular sovereignty rests on representation.

What must happen in elections if they are to generate popular sovereignty? We have already seen that they must allow voters to sanction incumbents whose past performance they do not approve of and reelect incumbents who have served them well. If elections do not serve this backward-looking sanctioning function, they lose their power to control incumbents' actions between elections. But elections must do more than this. They must also serve a forward-looking planning function, allowing citizens to evaluate alternative programs for the future. If campaigns do not indicate a general policy orientation of alternative future governments, then elections cannot communicate voters' preferences to governments. Furthermore, when voters decide whether to reelect or reject an incumbent, they must be able to evaluate the incumbent's performance against alternatives, and those alternatives are provided by the programs of challengers. If campaigns do not communicate alternatives, or if the alternatives communicated are not credible as general indications of future policy, voters will be stabbing in the dark when they reject incumbents in favor of challengers.

Elections do involve a planning function in many existing political systems. Evidence from the United States suggests that voters have both prospective and retrospective orientations: they use both the past performance of incumbents and the campaign messages of all competitors in deciding how to vote.[6] Furthermore, although I am unaware of systematic research on this topic, my sense is that in many political systems the general policy orientation of candidates announced in campaigns predicts reasonably well the general policy orientation of governments once in power. Although most governments will adopt particular policies not foreseen in campaigns and will break campaign promises, in many democracies it is rare that governments abandon their general orientation and pursue, say, that of a rival party. When they do change, as for example the French Socialists did after 1983, it tends to be after some time has elapsed and in response to clear changes in conditions. This practice, known as leapfrogging, is uncommon in Western European and North American systems, and immediate leapfrogging is virtually unknown.[7]

Some would claim that the nature of elections and electorates in all contemporary democracies severs the link between elections and popular sovereignty. Contemporary electorates even in advanced capitalist democracies are ill-informed about even the general policy orientations of candidates, and know too little about candidates' positions to use their vote as a way of signaling preferred policies.[8] A related though not identical claim is that voters lack an instrumental orientation in voting: they are motivated by emotions or symbols, or their vote expresses identification with inherent qualities of their preferred candidate (e.g., the candidate's gender, race, religion, ethnicity, political party, or the symbolic content of his or her rhetoric).[9]

However, even in the United States, where voters are notoriously ill-informed about candidates' policy positions, voting is still in part motivated by voters' policy preferences. Thus, Rabinowitz and MacDonald show that despite the poverty of US voters' knowledge of candidates' policy stances, voters tend to locate candidates on policy-relevant sides and to support the candidate located on the voter's own side.[10] Sniderman, Glaser, and Griffin find that policy preferences are one factor that informs electoral choice—indirectly among less-educated voters, and both directly and indirectly among well-educated voters.[11]

The ideal of popular sovereignty continues to underlie our enthusiasm for democracy over its modern alternatives, and it was this ideal that inspired early writings on the collapse of military rule in Latin America. During the long periods of military rule, decisions were taken by rulers whose authority was based on force, and who represented either no one but themselves or narrow, military-institutional interests, or the interests of a small elite. Even in countries such as Chile, where the military regime came to power with support among broad segments of the population, the people were not sovereign in any meaningful sense: the ongoing tenure of rulers did not depend on the ongoing support of those who initially had supported them, and rulers were not subject to the regular sanctions, formal and informal, that elected governments are.

The prodemocratic consensus in the early regime-transition literature reflected the belief that the opposite would be true of democratic governments. However wrongheaded their policies, however limited their abilities to right injustices and overcome social inequalities, at least they would be undergirded by the institutional infrastructure necessary for popular sovereignty. Elections would be a mechanism for the transmission of the interests and preferences of civil society into the policy-making process. Governmental terms punctuated by elections that either renewed the mandate of the party in power or sanctioned it by replacing one government with another meant that politicians' interest in power would be aligned with the public's interest in preferred policies.

I believe the early wave of writers was right in its comparative judgment of the greater potential for popular sovereignty in democratic as against military-authoritarian regimes. But the link between electoral systems and popular sovereignty in South America's new democracies has turned out to be more problematic than we thought. Looking closely at the tenuous connection between electoral outcomes and government policy, and at institutional settings that efface that connection, can teach us not only about contemporary Latin American democracies but about the conditions necessary, in general, for electoral systems to become systems of popular sovereignty.

The next section looks at some shifts in policies in South American countries.

Elections and Economic Policy Shifts

Five South American Cases

Argentina. During the early months of 1989, the outgoing Unión Cívica Radical (UCR) government of Raúl Alfonsín struggled against high (though not yet hyper) inflation, recession, and heavy international debt obligations. The presidential candidate from the ruling party, Eduardo Angeloz, distanced himself from some specific government policies and called for the resignation of economic minister Juan Sourrouille after the failure of a late 1988 emergency economic plan. Still, Angeloz called for "deepening" the economic achievements of the Alfonsín government, continued trade liberalization, good standing with international financial institutions, and privatization of state-owned enterprises.[12]

In July 1988, Carlos Menem, governor of La Rioja Province, defeated a reform precandidate, Peronist Party leader Antonio Cafiero, to become the Peronist (Partido Justicialista) presidential candidate. Menem's was a colorful campaign, with emphasis on his fondness for soccer, race cars, and fashion models. His economic message was nationalist and expansionist. He hinted early at a moratorium on foreign debt repayment, and although he shifted to favoring a five-year hiatus in payments with the approval of foreign creditors, he continued to make statements such as that he would not pay Argentina's foreign debt "by making the people go hungry."[13]

The Menem campaign coined the term *salariazo,* presumably a large upward shock to salaries and wages, in contrast to the *paquetazo,* the large upward shock to prices entailed in fiscal adjustments. Even as his party in congress was blocking the government's privatization efforts, Menem called for privatization only of inefficient firms, and ruled out privatizing utilities and the state-owned oil company.

Alvaro Alsogaray, the candidate of the conservative Unión del Centro Democrático (UCD), called for liberalized policies on trade, the exchange rate, and wages, and for speedy and full privatization and the honoring of standing agreements with international creditors.

Menem won the 14 May elections, taking 47 percent of the votes to Angeloz's 37 percent. Alsogaray placed a distant third with 6 percent.

The Alfonsín government—which was scheduled to remain in power for another seven months—announced a new set of economic measures four days after the election, but inflation continued to surge, reaching nearly 100 percent before month's end. Rioting and looting on 23 May left fourteen dead. The crisis produced an agreement between the government and Menem to move the transition forward from December to July.

Menem's cabinet, announced in July, contained surprises. The economic minister would be Miguel Roig, a former vice-president of Bunge y Born, Argentina's largest multinational firm and "an outstanding symbol of *vendepatria* [sellout] capitalism to all Peronists, both elites and masses."[14] When Roig died eleven days after assuming his post, Menem replaced him with another Bunge y Born vice-president, Néstor Rapanelli. Menem's labor minister was Jorge Triaca, a conservative labor figure. Triaca's appointment and the government's emerging economic policies precipitated a split in the Peronist labor confederation, the Confederación General de Trabajadores (CGT), and the formation of an antigovernment wing of the CGT under Saúl Ubaldini. Equally surprising was Menem's appointment to various posts of Julia Alsogaray, daughter of UCD candidate Álvaro Alsogaray and herself an UCD leader. Among her new positions was that of director of the state telephone company, an enterprise she soon privatized. Her father, Álvaro Alsogaray, went to Washington to serve as the Peronist government's negotiator with Argentina's international creditors.

Menem's economic policies bore a close resemblance to those advocated by Alsogaray in the campaign. The Bunge y Born Plan (as it was known) included a sharp fiscal adjustment, a 170 percent devaluation of the austral, privatization of telecommunications, the state airlines, television and radio stations, petrochemicals, and steel, and the phasing out of export taxes and import tariffs.[15] Menem, the author of the concept of salariazo, prepared Argentines for price adjustments in August 1989 by calling for "a tough, costly, and severe adjustment" requiring "major surgery without anesthesia."[16]

Peru. Peru's 1990 presidential campaign took place in the midst of high inflation brought on during the administration of Alain García. The economy was the focus of the campaign, and all candidates made pronouncements about how to end the crisis. On one side was the unusually open neoliberalism of Mario Vargas Llosa, who laid out in detail his approach to stabilization: quickly reduce the budget deficit by eliminating subsidies and public services, by increasing the price of public-sector goods, and by reducing the number of public employees; hold back growth of the money supply by raising real interest rates and eliminating loans from the central bank to the government. Stabilization, said Vargas Llosa, must be accompanied by market-oriented reforms: unification of exchange rates, currency devaluation and liberalization, tariff reductions, and privatization of public enterprises and utilities. Both stabilization and structural reforms would be painful in the short term, reducing real incomes and increasing unemployment. To shield the most vulnerable from these painful effects, Vargas Llosa proposed an emergency antipoverty fund. As a FREDEMO slogan put it, "It will cost us, but together we will make the Great Change."

In contrast to Vargas Llosa's approach to stabilization and economic reform, various candidates proposed more gradualist remedies to monetary and balance-of-payments disequilibria, and more statist approaches to long-term economic reform. Out of this field, Alberto Fujimori, an independent and relative unknown, emerged to place a strong second behind Vargas Llosa in the April first round.[17] A team of center-left economists hurriedly elaborated Fujimori's platform between the first and second round of the election in June. The platform proposed stabilization "without recession . . . protecting throughout the period of adjustment the buying power of workers and assuring that the costs of the transition be equitably distributed."[18] The plan envisioned a "debureaucratized" state, but one that would help enhance productivity through human capital and infrastructure investments. The plan also called for respect for property rights, for job security, and labor rights. Fujimori's program stressed negotiated agreements with key sectors to achieve price stability and reforms. It called for dialogue between the state, unions, and business, a "Social Pact for Development," to increase productivity and generate a more equal distribution of resources. On the campaign trail, Fujimori condensed these proposals into themes and slogans. The most salient was his gradualist, "antishock" approach to fighting inflation.

Fujimori won the second round of the election by 57 percent to Vargas Llosa's 35 percent (8 percent of ballots were invalid). Fujimori's chief sources of electoral strength were the urban and rural lower classes, and he had the formal support of Peru's major leftist and center-left parties. Fujimori was inaugurated on Peru's independence day, 28 July, 1990.

In a televised address eleven days later, Fujimori's economic minister, Juan Carlos Hurtado Miller, announced price adjustments on gasoline, basic foodstuffs, and public services of between 200 percent and 500 percent. If Fujimori's "shock" involved price adjustments larger than those Vargas Llosa had laid out in his campaign, Fujimori's longer-term economic reforms were much like those Vargas Llosa had proposed: exchange rate unification and liberalization, reduction and simplification of tariffs on imports, elimination of tariffs on exports, capital market liberalization, tax reform, reduction of employees in government and state-owned enterprises, privatization of state-owned enterprises and financial institutions, elimination of job security laws, elimination of wage indexation, liberalization of labor relations, and privatization of social security. Gone was any sense of policy implementation through "concertation" or negotiations with the representatives of labor and business. Concertation took on a new meaning in the progovernment press: it came to describe after-the-fact policy decisions to businessmen, economists, and the Roman Catholic Church, the last increasingly the only representative of social concerns with whom the government was willing to communicate.[19]

Ecuador. In Ecuador we will consider two cases of policy shift. The promise to forego a surprise, dramatic fiscal adjustment—*el antishock* as it was known in Peru—was a common element in both of that country's two most recent presidential campaigns. Nevertheless, exactly such an adjustment occurred in the early days of each new administration.

In 1988, Rodrigo Borja, candidate of the social-democratic Izquierda Democrática (ID), announced that his government would abandon the neoliberal orientation of the ruling administration of León Febres Cordero. There would be no privatizations, concertation agreements would be reached between the government, labor, and business, and there would be no surprise fiscal adjustments. It was said that "corrective measures would be taken against corruption, not against production" and all changes would be "progressive [i.e., incremental] and pre-programmed."[20]

Three weeks after winning the second round of the election Borja announced the "shock." The price of fuel rose by 100 percent, electricity by 30 percent. The sucre was devalued by 75 percent to

390 sucres to the dollar, and weekly devaluations of 2.5 sucres would follow (the "crawling peg"). The impact of the measures on workers would be offset partially by a 16 percent increase in the minimum wage (but the monthly inflation rate averaged 4.7 percent in the four months after the September adjustment). The announced aim of the package was to save US$450 million in foreign reserves by December, to reduce inflation from 57 percent to 30 percent, and to achieve a 7 percent GDP growth rate (the economy had grown 5.5 percent in 1987). Borja's change of course was forced upon him, he said, by "the financial bankruptcy, the economic disorder, the administrative corruption, and the fiscal crisis" left by the outgoing Febres Cordero government, the proportions of which had not been known before.[21]

Four years later, in 1992, the two highest vote-getters in the first round of Ecuador's presidential elections were Jaime Nebot, of the conservative Social Christian Party (PSC), and Sixto Durán, representing an alliance of the center-right Unified Republican Party (PRE) and the Conservative Party of Ecuador (PCE). Nebot was seen as the more radically neoliberal of the two candidates, whereas Durán cultivated a grandfatherly image. Both campaigns fought to stigmatize one another as planning a shock—a surprise price adjustment. Durán claimed to favor an approach to price stabilization "far from the 'shock' and from gradualism." He also announced that his government would lower the price of medicines "which is what poor people need most." It would also sponsor a massive program of construction of low-cost housing, "substantial" education reforms, and the extension of medical services and hospitals.[22]

That particular year, 1992, in Ecuador was a moment of reaction against the center-left government of Borja. Both Durán and Nebot were conservatives, and if voters found Durán's moderately expansionist campaign message to be credible, they might have been expected to have interpreted the presence on the ticket of Alberto Dahik, Durán's running mate, as an indication that a Durán presidency would signify an orthodox approach to stabilization and structural reform. Dahik was an economist of monetarist orientation who had served as the president of the Junta Monetaria under Febres Cordero. Still, during the campaign Dahik specialized in denying Nebot's claim, repeated in TV and radio advertising, that Durán planned a shock that would include doubling the price of gasoline.

Durán won the second round of the election in July, and on 3 September announced price adjustments including a 125 percent increase in the price of gasoline, an average doubling of electricity rates, and a 35.5 percent devaluation of the sucre. The structural reforms, or Nuevo Rumbo, had a familiar ring. They included a reduction of government spending, a freeze on public-sector employment, the elimination or fusion of some small public agencies, incentives for early retirement in the public sector, a onetime tax on businesses, an exchange rate that would float (after the onetime devaluation) within a fixed range, a market-determined interest rate, and restraint in the increase of the money supply. The plan's aim was to reduce the budget deficit to 3 percent of GDP, to bring foreign reserves up to US$500 million by December, and to reduce inflation, which would start to decline six to eight months after the plan was announced.[23]

The plan also included a "program of social compensation." Price hikes on electricity would not affect small users, and bus drivers would be compensated so that fares would not rise.[24] Salary increases approved in July (under the outgoing Borja administration) would be respected, and a "16th salary" (a monthly bonus promised in the campaign) would be established.

Bolivia. In 1985, Bolivia was in the grips of hyperinflation, running at an annual rate of 23,000 percent, as well as sharp political and social conflict, when president Hernán Siles Suazo agreed to hold elections more than a year ahead of schedule. General Hugo Banzer was the candidate of the right-wing Alianza Democrática Nacional (ADN), the party he had founded in 1978. Banzer espoused a neoliberal approach to stabilization and reform, and closely associated himself with prominent members of the business community. He was also publicly associated with Jeffrey Sachs, Harvard economist and advisor to many governments undertaking liberalizing reforms. Banzer, who had headed a military regime between 1974 and 1979, was also regarded as the more likely candidate to repress those who resisted his policies.

Víctor Paz Estenssoro was the candidate of the Movimiento Nacional Revolucionario (MNR), the protagonist of Bolivia's 1952 revolution. Paz Estenssoro's economic policy pronouncements were mixed. For the mass public he employed what was described as a "traditional populist discourse."[25] But in front of some audiences, Paz signaled plans for a tough anti-inflation program. In an April 1985 forum organized by the La Paz Chamber of Commerce, he called for a harsh program of fiscal adjustment and promised to negotiate an agreement with the International Monetary Fund (IMF). Despite these mixed signals, judging from history and campaign messages, analysts, and probably voters, saw Paz Estenssoro as occupying a centrist or even "populist" position vis-à-vis Banzer's more aggressive neoliberalism.[26]

Banzer placed first in the July 1985 elections with 28 percent of the popular vote, Paz Estenssoro second with 26 percent. Jaime Paz Zamora of the Movimiento de Izquierda Revolucionaria (MIR) finished third with a surprisingly large 9 percent (surprising given that Paz Zamora was the vice-president of the outgoing Unidad Democrática Popular—UDP—government).

We do not know with precision the profile of MNR versus ADN supporters in the 1985 elections. Voting results by electoral district show that Banzer's ADN had urban support, dominating voting in La Paz and in provincial capitals, whereas Paz Estenssoro's support came from rural communities.[27] The MNR's role in the 1952 revolution, in promoting agrarian reform and in founding the COB (Bolivian Labor Confederation), probably made for lasting support among peasants and workers.

The Bolivian constitution requires congress to elect a president from among the three highest vote-getters when no candidate receives an absolute majority of the popular vote (a likely result, given the large number of political parties). After complex negotiations, Paz Estenssoro was elected president on 6 August with the support in congress of the MIR and smaller left-wing parties.

Two weeks after assuming the presidency, Paz Estenssoro implemented a stabilization program that included price adjustments like those proposed by Banzer during his campaign, accompanied by structural reforms that would fundamentally reorient the Bolivian economy—reducing the fiscal deficit and the size of the state, eliminating subsidies on state-controlled goods and public services, privatizing key sectors such as mining, reducing barriers to international trade, and liberalizing the exchange rate, interest rates, and other prices. These measures, contained in Supreme Decree 21060, laid out the New Economic Program (NPE) that over the following eight years would amount to a neoliberal revolution.

Not only was the content of the NPE very close to the economic reforms that Banzer had proposed in the campaign, but the repressive policy style that Paz used to enforce the reforms was probably close to the style Banzer would have used had he been elected. Indeed, it would have been hard to implement the NPE without resistance in a country with Bolivia's history of labor union activism. The COB called a series of strikes in response to the measures and the government sought to impose a state of siege to confront the strike. But Paz Estenssoro's leftist MIR allies in congress opposed the state of siege. Thus, in September 1985 the MNR broke with the left and signed a "pact for democracy" with the ADN. The governing alliance was based on common support for the NPE and for harsh measures against labor. The state of siege duly imposed, 143 labor leaders were sent to detainment camps in the Amazonian jungle.

Explaining Policy Shift

In four of the five cases examined in the previous section, majority preferences in economic policy, as expressed in elections, failed to translate into government policy.[28] Instead, governments appeared quick to implement the preferred policy of a minority of voters.[29] I use the term *quick* advisedly: in each case, the adoption of the minority-preferred policy occurred immediately the new president assumed power, making it unlikely that changed economic conditions led governments to abandon their apparently mandated policies. These elections failed, then, to serve a planning function: candidates supplied general but clearly alternative approaches to economic policy, but these approaches were not firm prior commitments. Campaign plans mapped poorly onto government actions.

To understand why mandated policies were abandoned it is helpful to know *when* they were abandoned. The Argentine and Peruvian cases, for which my information is fullest, show that sometimes candidates had clear plans before the election to abandon their campaign pledges and sometimes they had no such clear intentions. In an interview I conducted in April 1993, Julio Bárbaro, a Menem campaign official, told me that Menem made the decision to turn the economic ministry over to Bunge y Born immediately after he defeated Cafiero in the Peronist internal elections, a full year before assuming office. Four years after the election, Menem conceded to a journalist that he had hidden his intentions to privatize the telephone company, airline, and railways, and to resume diplomatic ties with Britain, because he feared the wrath of voters and of labor unions.[30]

In Peru, on the other hand, interviews with a number of former Fujimori campaign advisors painted a picture of a dark-horse candidate dead set on winning an election that he appeared to have no chance of winning as of four weeks before the first round. His economist advisors wrote plans that were well considered and elaborate. The candidate, himself an academic mathematician and a quick learner, understood their plans, in their view, fully. Fujimori may have intuited that he might have to depart from campaign commitments, in particular *el anti-shock*, but he had no specific plans to do so.[31] The change of course was a product of the transition period after the second round of the elections and before the change of government.

In Bolivia, Paz Estenssoro's mixed economic policy signals, which included his statement before the business forum that he would impose austerity measures, suggest some intention to abandon the more populist side of his campaign proposals, placing him closer to the Menem dissimulated-intentions position than to the Fujimori postelection, change-of-course position. In Ecuador, a member of Durán's cabinet conceded to me in an interview that the Durán government's policies were at odds with the ones announced in the campaign, and said that if these intentions had been announced, Durán would have lost the election.[32] Durán's alliance before the election with the monetarist Alberto Dahik, even given Dahik's anti-austerity protestations, is further evidence of campaign dissimulation. In the earlier case in Ecuador— the case of Rodrigo Borja—it seems that the ID party program had great weight in setting policy. This is suggested by the fact that Borja made only one departure from the economic policy intentions he announced during his campaign: the fiscal shock. I do not know whether that single departure was preplanned or whether, as the new president claimed, new information induced the change after he assumed power.

Why did new governments impose policies radically different from those mandated by electoral majorities?[33] The answer, I believe, is as follows. Candidates perceived that a majority of voters preferred security-oriented policies, particularly ones that avoided high unemployment over policies of rapid stabilization of prices and current accounts. Campaign messages and the inherited political culture structured the alternatives in this way in the minds of voters. Or, using Rabinowitz and MacDonald's language, voters saw one major candidate as on the side of protecting employment at the cost of slower stabilization, and the other major candidate on the side of lowering inflation and correcting trade imbalances at the cost of high unemployment. The winning candidates accurately saw most voters as favoring security. The losing candidate was either (1) ideologically so committed to being pro-stabilization that he could not depart from it even though this meant losing the election, or (2) he wished to inject his perspective into the political culture even at the cost of losing the current election, or (3) he misjudged the preferences of the electorate and his own ability to persuade.[34] But if the electoral logic operated in favor of security-oriented policies, the logic of power operated in favor of radical stabilization policies. Candidates who foresaw this shifting political-economic logic during campaigns dissimulated; those who discovered it after gaining office made an unanticipated change of policy course.

Three explanations would account for the shifting logic. First, when structural adjustment programs work, their benefits are typically felt after several years of recession. Politicians may have thought that, although orthodox stabilization would leave the majority of people better off by the next election, voters myopically focused only on the painful short-term effects. If the economy could be expected to improve, politicians would expect voters' preferences to shift as a result of the policy.[35]

A second possible explanation is that new presidents perceived that powerful economic agents (i.e., their domestic bourgeoisies and the international financial institutions) strongly favored orthodox stabilization and would impose economic sanctions that could make life difficult for politicians and their constituents. In the first scenario, presidents believed voters were myopic in failing to foresee the future economic benefits of following orthodox reforms; in the second, voters were myopic in failing to perceive the hardship imposed by powerful actors if their government did not pursue orthodox reforms.

A third possible explanation is that politicians did not see voters as myopic but understood them to be deciding to trade off rapid stabilization in favor of greater security, particularly lower unemployment. Politicians were offered incentives by domestic and international economic interests that were sufficiently attractive for them to abandon mandated policies, even at the risk of dimming their future electoral prospects. In theory, if politicians valued both the power of office and, say, its financial rewards, bribes alone, if they were of a sufficiently high level, could purchase the abandonment of mandated policies, even if doing so meant sure loss of office. Inducements more relevant to our cases were international prestige, reduced effort at negotiations, and the prospect of generalized political support in an uncertain future.[36]

I believe that pressure from domestic and international economic interests, uncertainty about the results of any policy, and a perception of unstable and manipulable voter preferences all played a role in producing policy change. The fact that all of these governments are considered by many economists to have overdone stabilization policies suggests that politicians were not convinced by the technical superiority of orthodox reforms (in which case they would have followed mainstream economic advice closely), but were attempting to signal loudly their compliance to domestic markets and foreign creditors.[37] Furthermore, when new presidents were pressed by international financial institutions and economists to change policy course, the communication tended to be political, not technical.

Thus, Peru's Alberto Fujimori spent a few hours in a meeting with the heads of multilateral lending institutions in July 1990 and was told, in essence: Abandon your campaign policies or you will not get any support from us. After receiving the same message from Japan's prime minister, Fujimori returned to Peru with a new policy.

Menem's alliance with the UCD's Álvaro and Julia Alsogaray appeared designed not to pursue Alsogaray's electoral bases, which were narrow (6 percent of voters supported Álvaro Alsogaray in the 1989 elections). Instead, Menem wished to send calming signals to domestic markets and international financial institutions and governments. In Ecuador, Pablo Lucio Paredes, Durán's minister of planning, told me in an interview in February 1993 with some pleasure that the draconian quality of the Nuevo Rumbo had surprised the IMF, especially in the program's ambitious deficit-reduction measures, which went beyond IMF targets.

In sum, new presidents desired prestige in international and elite domestic circles, feared sanctions from these circles, and were uncertain enough about the outcome of any set of economic policies (and about voter behavior at later elections) that they decided to bend with the wind of elite preferences, to hope economic outcomes would be favorable, and to try to manipulate public opinion in ways that would limit whatever damage the policy shift and unpopular policies caused.

This explanation focuses attention on the political and institutional features likely to make politicians less concerned with future elections, voter preferences less stable, and voters less able to discern the likely effects of alternative policies and the real opportunities and constraints operating on politicians. In the next three sections I list several institutional features that may influence the level of consistency between voter preferences and policy. Only further research will establish their relevance.

Anticipating Future Elections

Repeated elections and reelectability. In Peru, Argentina, and Bolivia, although the office of the presidency was filled by repeated election, incumbent presidents were required to wait one term before seeking the presidency again. If the anticipation of future elections was to discipline politicians, these officeholders would either have to have a long time perspective (and to think voters had long memories) or they would have to be strongly motivated to pursue party reelection. Ecuadorian presidents were barred from ever seeking reelection; reelection of their party was the only future electoral consideration that would weigh on incumbent presidents in Ecuador.

Even if standing presidents wished to have their party retain the presidency at the next election, and even if they could and did entertain long-term electoral aspirations, it is difficult to believe the next election would not have been more present in their minds had immediate reelection been possible.[38]

Voters' Ability to Discern

Majority status. Powell argues that to hold politicians accountable, voters have to be able to ascribe responsibility for policies to particular governmental actors.[39] He notes that it is easiest for voters to ascribe responsibility when a single party occupies the executive and a majority of legislative seats; that it is more difficult when an alliance of parties established before the election controls the executive and legislature; that it is more difficult still when a postelection alliance is in power; and that it is most difficult of all under a minority government. At the time the unmandated policies were imposed, in two of the five governments discussed in this chapter (Menem's and Borja's) the ruling party alone had a near-majority in the legislature (49.6 percent and 47.5 percent of seats, respectively), and could expect congressional support on most issues. In a third (Paz Estenssoro's) the two distinct postelection alliances (MNR-MIR and MNR-ADN) both enjoyed absolute majorities. In the two other cases discussed here (Fujimori's and Durán's), minority governments relied on issue-by-issue alliances for legislative support.

Given the inordinate power of the president in all these countries, however, are voters likely to be confused or misled by divided governments? Although we might think of extreme presidential power as leaving presidents unconstrained, if voters were aware of that power they would tend to ascribe policy responsibility where it is due—to presidents. But the dominance of presidents will not facilitate voter discernment if voters can be misled as to which president is responsible. New presidents, in justifying the abandonment of mandated policies, blamed not legislatures but outgoing presidents, and in at least two cases, the voters believed them.[40]

The Stability of Preferences

Parties and the political class. Political parties and party systems in all countries discussed here except Argentina were weak and shifting;

in democracies where elections appear to fulfill a planning function, parties are stronger and more stable.

Even outside of Latin America, governments run by strong and enduring political parties have embarked on policy shifts; an example is Bob Hawke's 1983 Labour government in Australia. Only further research will reveal whether the Argentine and Australian cases are exceptions to a general association between strong party systems and elections that serve a planning function.

Why might weak parties undermine the planning function of elections, and thus undermine popular sovereignty? Western European political parties have been shown to educate their constituents' policy preferences, staking out relatively extreme positions on the same side as their constituents and defining latent political identities.[41] Strong, enduring political parties may create a more stable environment for public opinion, leaving voters less prone to shifts in preferences over time.

In addition to creating stable voter preferences, parties cultivate technical cadre—people capable of prescribing and implementing complex measures that are consistent with the political mandate provided by voters. All of the five governments discussed here turned for technical advice to a floating group of "technopols," whose policy orientation was aligned with that of domestic and international elites.[42] Hernando de Soto became a dominant member of Fujimori's transition team in July 1990; de Soto had been a close associate of Vargas Llosa, sharing the podium with Vargas Llosa at the 1987 mass rally that in effect initiated Vargas Llosa's campaign. Fujimori's first economic minister, Juan Carlos Hurtado Miller was a prominent member of Acción Popular, one of the member parties of the FREDEMO coalition that backed Vargas Llosa. Although Hurtado was not active in FREDEMO, it is a safe bet that he voted for Vargas Llosa. Carlos Boloña, Fujimori's second and more important economic minister, was a World Bank economist who was likely to have supported Vargas Llosa in the elections.

The team that designed Bolivia's New Economic Program (NPE) was made up of eight members, mainly economists and businessmen. The only member of the team who was also a member of the MNR was Gonzálo Sánchez de Lozada (he is also a businessman). Juan Carriaga, a team member who would eventually become finance minister, served as the bridge between the team and Jeffrey Sachs, the erstwhile advisor to Paz Estenssoro's opponent, General Banzer. This team, which worked intensely between 8 August 1985 (two days after Paz Estenssoro's election in congress) and 29 August (the day the

NPE was announced) was in stark contrast with Paz's official cabinet, named on 7 August. The cabinet was made up exclusively of MNR members, all of them figures of little stature within the party. This cabinet was easily replaced, largely by members of the behind-the-scenes economic team, after the first, contentious months of stabilization.

In Ecuador, under Durán, all cabinet posts involving economic policy were held by former officials in the government of León Febres Cordero (1984–1988), the former president from the Partido Social Cristiano (PSC) of Jaime Nebot, Durán's opponent in the election. Thus, Pablo Lucio Paredes, Durán's planning minister, had been an advisor to the Junta Monetaria under Febres Cordero; Mario Ribadeneira, Durán's minister of finance, was Febres's ambassador to Washington; and Ana Lucía Armijos, Durán's Central bank chief, had been the head of monetary policy at the bank under Febres. Durán himself had been the PSC vice-president under Febres (he left the party after winning only 10 percent of the vote as the PSC presidential candidate in 1988). But in the 1992 campaign, Durán opposed the dramatic shift toward neoliberalism that the Febres government had pursued. In an interview in February 1993, I asked Paredes if there was not something odd about all of Durán's key economic posts going to people who had worked in the most recent administration of the party that had just lost the elections. He responded that there was nothing at all odd in all this: they had broken with Febres—as had the president—and they were now carrying out the policies they had always favored. We pursue the same policies, he seemed to be saying, without interference from the electorate.

Conclusions

We have seen that citizens must be presented with at least the outlines of alternative policies, outlines that serve as credible maps of real government action, if elections are to support popular sovereignty. In several South American countries, losing policy proposals served as better maps of policy than did winning ones.

My provisional explanation of this phenomenon focused on foreign and domestic elite pressure, uncertainty of economic outcomes, and the perception of voter myopia or manipulability. I suggested political and institutional features that may have undermined the planning function of elections: limits on presidential reelection, frequent nonmajority governments, and weak political parties.

Whatever the exact explanation for why these elections failed to serve a planning function, it is clear that the unconstrained policy preferences of the majority of voters were at odds with the preferred policies of domestic bourgeoisies, international financial interests, and foreign political elites. The information presented here cannot disconfirm the hypothesis that politicians abandoned mandated policies because they thought the unmandated policies were better for voters (and that voters would judge them to be better retrospectively), quite apart from foreign and elite preferences and threatened sanctions. But I have offered evidence suggesting that elite pressure and the perception of voter manipulability, rather than the perception that unmandated policies were better for voters, lay behind the change of course in most of these cases. To the extent that this is generally true, policy shift in several of South America's new democracies reveals a tension between popular sovereignty and dependent capitalism. The fact that domestic political power originated with the people, and that the people sometime in the future would choose again, was insufficient to hold politicians to the people's preferred policy course.

Notes

This chapter was first presented at the Sixteenth World Congress of the International Political Science Association, Berlin, 21–25 August 1994. Research was supported by the MacArthur Foundation–SSRC Program in International Peace and Security.

1. Guillermo O'Donnell, Philippe Schmitter, and Laurence Whitehead, eds. *Transitions from Authoritarian Rule: Prospects for Democracy*, 4 vols. (Baltimore: Johns Hopkins University Press, 1986); Larry Diamond, Juan Linz, and Seymour Martin Lipset, *Democracy in Developing Countries: Latin America* (Boulder: Lynne Rienner, 1989); James A. Malloy and Mitchell A. Seligson, *Authoritarians and Democrats: Regime Transitions in Latin America* (Pittsburgh: University of Pittsburgh Press, 1987); Abraham Lowenthal, ed., *Exporting Democracy: The United States and Latin America* (Baltimore: Johns Hopkins University Press, 1989).

2. Guillermo O'Donnell and Philippe Schmitter, *Transitions from Authoritarian Rule: Tentative Conclusions About Uncertain Democracies* (Baltimore: Johns Hopkins University Press, 1986), p. 3.

3. See, for example, Guillermo O'Donnell, "Delegative Democracy?" Kellogg Institute working paper 172, March 1992; Francisco Weffort, "New Democracies, Which Democracies?" Woodrow Wilson Center Latin American Program working paper 198, 1992; Marcelo Cavarozzi, "Beyond Transitions to Democracy in Latin America," paper presented at Congress of Latin American Studies Association, 1991; L. Paramio, "Problemas en la consolidación democrática en América Latina en los '90," *Nexos*, no. 169, Dec. 1991;

and S. Zermeño, "El regreso del lider: crisis, neoliberalismo y desorden," *Revista Mexicana de Sociología*, no. 4, 1989.

4. The first view was that of James Madison, the second of Emmanuel Siéyès. Both are cited in Bernard Manin, "The Metamorphoses of Representative Government," *Economy and Society* 23, no. 2, May 1994, pp. 133–171. See Manin's discussion of the partial independence of representatives under parliamentary government, ibid., p. 8ff.

5. Burke claimed that trustee-legislators with a "communion of interests and a sympathy in feelings and desires" could be trusted to act in the name of the people "though the trustees are not actually chosen by them." Cited in Hannah Fenichel Pitkin, ed., *The Concept of Representation* (New York: Atherton, 1969), p. 169.

6. See Paul M. Sniderman, James M. Glaser, and Robert Griffin, "Information and Electoral Choice," in John A. Ferejohn and James H. Kuklinski, eds., *Information and Democratic Processes* (Urbana: University of Illinois Press, 1990), 117–135.

7. There is, however, the case of the 1983 policy switch of Bob Hawke's government in Australia—at least one instance of immediate and drastic policy switch in an OECD country/West European–style parliamentary system.

8. Joseph Schumpeter rejected representational theories of democracy partly on these grounds. He found incredible the idea that "'the people' hold a definite and rational opinion about every individual question and that they give effect to this opinion—in a democracy—by choosing 'representatives' who will see to it that that opinion is carried out." *Capitalism, Socialism and Democracy*, 3d edition (New York: Harper, 1950), p. 269.

9. See Maurice Edelman, *The Symbolic Uses of Politics* (Urbana and Chicago: University of Illinois Press, 1967).

10. George Rabinowitz and Stuart E. MacDonald, "A Directional Theory of Issue Voting," *American Political Science Review* 83, no. 1, 1989, pp. 93–121. See also Torben Iversen, "The Logics of Electoral Politics: Spatial, Directional, and Mobilizational Effects," *Comparative Political Studies* 27, no. 2, pp. 155–189, 1994.

11. Sniderman, Glaser, and Griffin, ibid.

12. For a summary of the three leading candidates' economic policy positions, see *Clarín*, "Suplemento Económico," 23 April 1989, p. 6.

13. Cited in Mary Schuler, "An Inquiry into the Logic Behind President Carlos Menem's Policy Shift After the 1989 Argentine Presidential Elections," manuscript, University of Chicago, 1994, p. 10.

14. William C. Smith, "State, Market and Neoliberalism in Post-Transition Argentina: The Menem Experiment," *Journal of Interamerican Studies and World Affairs* 33, no. 4 (1991), p. 52.

15. For details on this and subsequent Peronist government economic programs during the government's first two years, see Smith, ibid., pp. 53–65.

16. Ibid., p. 53.

17. Peru's 1979 constitution required a runoff election between the two highest vote-getters if no candidate received more than 50 percent of votes. The 1993 constitution has the same requirement.

18. *Cambio '90*, "Lineamientos del Plan de Gobierno 1990," p. 10.

19. See, for example, "Boloña firma con Banco Mundial créditos pro US$1.150 millones," *Expreso*, Lima (22 December 1992).

20. Quoted in *Latin American Weekly Report*—Andean Group, London, 3 March 1988, and 23 June 1988, respectively.

21. From Borja's broadcast speech announcing price adjustments, quoted in *El Comercio*, Quito, 31 August 1988.

22. Cited in Diego Cornejo Menacho, "Los 100 Días de Durán-Dahik," *Ecuador Debate*, no. 27, December 1992, pp. 9–10. Inflation at the time of the campaign was running at an annual rate of 52 percent—high by Ecuadorian standards.

23. *Ecuador: Plan Macroeconómico de Estabilización*, Banco Central de Ecuador, September 1992.

24. Increases in bus fares, especially for students, have traditionally sparked rioting in Latin America.

25. René Antonio Mayorga, "La Democracia en Bolivia: El Rol de las Elecciones en las Fases de Transición y Consolidación," in Rodolfo Cerdas-Cruz et al., eds., *Elecciones y Democracia en América Latina, 1988–1991*, San Juan, Costa Rica: IIDH-CAPEL, 1992, p. 251.

26. Mayorga, ibid., and social scientists and campaign advisors whom I interviewed in March 1993 perceived this as the relative positioning of the candidates at the time of the election and believed voters shared this perception. Unfortunately, there is little polling of public opinion in Bolivia. Polls conducted during the campaign and after the election were for the use of campaigns and government and were not available for inspection.

27. See Mayorga, ibid., p. 257.

28. The degree of inconsistency between campaign pronouncements and policy is not identical in the five cases. In further research, I will attempt to quantify the degree of inconsistency in these and all other Latin American governments from 1982 to the present. I anticipate Menem and Fujimori will rank high in inconsistency, Paz Estenssoro and Durán somewhat lower, and Borja lowest. The Dominican Republic's Salvador Jorge Blanco (1982–1988) may attain a score as high as Menem's and Fujimori's; Venezuela's Carlos Andrés Pérez (1989–1993) and Jamaica's Michael Manley (1989–1993) may rank with Durán and Paz Estenssoro.

29. Only Paz Estenssoro was adopting a program and policy style of an opponent, Hugo Banzer, who had actually won the elections in terms of the popular vote (but by a very small margin). It is conceivable that Paz Estenssoro's strategy was to win over the loyalties of Banzer voters by adopting their preferred policies. Even in the unlikely case that he would thus lose all of his supporters, his MNR would come out ahead numerically. I believe it is more likely, however, that the situation inducing policy shift in Estenssoro's Bolivia was not fundamentally different from the situation in the other cases described here.

30. *Gente*, 4 January 1993, cited in José Nun, "Postmodern Politics? The Paradoxes of Peronism," paper prepared for the First Vienna Dialogue on Democracy, July 7–10, 1994, pp. 22–23.

31. In an interview, Fernando Villarán, a former campaign advisor, told me that he had been suspicious of candidate Fujimori's dogged insistence on *el anti-shock*. Some adjustment is coming, Villarán told him, so you shouldn't place so much weight on the antishock. "Think more like a statesman, not only like a politician," Villarán reported having told the candidate. Fujimori replied, "If I don't think like a politician now, I'll never get to be a statesman."

32. Interview with Pablo Lucio Paredes, February 1993.

33. For a more elaborate discussion of the causes of policy change, see Susan Stokes, "Democratic Accountability and Policy Change: Economic Policy in Fujimori's Peru," manuscript, University of Chicago, 1994.

34. The three are not mutually exclusive. From his memoirs, it is clear that Peru's Mario Vargas Llosa wanted to win the 1990 election, but he also wanted to introduce a neoliberal paradigm, in which he believed deeply, into mass political thinking. He did not perceive these two goals to be incompatible, but reading the memoir, my sense is that, had he done so, he would not have softened his message. See *El Pez en el Agua: Memorias* (Barcelona: Seix Barral, 1993).

35. In a May 1994 interview, I asked Roberto Dromi, Menem's first minister of public works (1989–1990) and a key actor in the privatization program, why Menem had hidden his economic policy intentions in the 1989 campaign, for example, by speaking of a moratorium on debt repayments and of the salariazo. He responded that not to speak of a salariazo would have meant alienating workers in the public sector, who made up 10 percent of the country's economically active population. But, he added, austerity measures were required to control inflation. Why, I responded, did Menem not advocate austerity to reduce inflation, thus appealing to the 90 percent of the population who were not public sector employees? At this point he read to me a passage from Machiavelli's *The Prince:* "new laws" will be the most difficult to enact, because they meet the resistance of all those who benefited from the former laws, and only tepid support from those who will benefit from the new laws. This support is tepid because the beneficiaries of new laws are afraid of the beneficiaries of the old, and because of the "incredulity of men, who never trust new things until they see their fruits." (Dromi cites these passages, from chapters XXVI and VI of *The Prince*, in the epigraph to his *Estado Nuevo, Nuevo Derecho* [Buenos Aires: Ediciones Ciudad Argentina, 1994]).

However confident Menemist insiders were about the retrospective approval of voters for reforms that they would support only tepidly, Dromi also made clear that the government's early actions were meant to "send a clear signal" to international actors. He named as intended receivers of those signals the US government and several international banks that are Argentina's creditors.

36. These three explanations are not exhaustive. For example, a common claim justifying unannounced fiscal adjustments was that they were forced by current-account deficits that the outgoing administration hid. There is some plausibility to this claim for the Brazil of 1985. See Luiz Carlos Bresser Pereira, José María Maravall, and Adam Przeworski, *Economic Reforms in New Democracies: A Social-Democratic Approach* (Cambridge: Cambridge University Press, 1993), p. 47. But the explanation is less plausible in other cases. For instance, in Ecuador the Durán government claimed that the budget deficit it found upon coming to office was 7 percent of GNP, whereas the outgoing Borja government claimed it was 3 percent. The truth, according to independent accounts, lay somewhere in the middle, and Durán used some unorthodox accounting methods to exaggerate the deficit to justify the surprise fiscal adjustment. The Fujimori administration made the same claim, although foreign pressure and not new information about deficits induced the shock.

37. In particular, these governments ignored economists' advice to sequence their reforms (e.g., to address fiscal deficits and macroeconomic imbalances before embarking on trade liberalization). See Cesar Martinelli and Mariano Tommasi, "Sequencing of Economic Reforms in the Presence of Political Constraints," UCLA WP 701, July 1993.

38. The recent shift toward immediate reelectability of presidents in Argentina and Peru will have the effect of tightening the link between presidents and voters.

39. G. Bingham Powell, Jr., "Holding Governments Accountable: How Constitutional Arrangements and Party Systems Affect Clarity of Responsibility for Policy in Contemporary Democracies." Paper presented at the meetings of the American Political Science Association, San Francisco, 1990.

40. In Lima, a September 1990 poll by *Cambio '90* found 63 percent of respondents who reported having voted agreeing with the following statement: "Fujimori didn't plan a shock, but once in office found no alternative." In contrast, 69 percent of Vargas Llosa supporters thought the president "tricked" voters when he said there would be no shock. The poll of 529 respondents was conducted by Apoyo, S.A.. In Ecuador in 1988, a poll taken just after Borja's *paquetazo* found 49 percent of respondents approved of the measures and 68 percent believed that they were inevitable (even though a poll just before the measures found 70 percent of respondents opposed to increases smaller than the one the government eventually imposed). The polls were taken by Informe Confidencial, with random samples of four hundred adults in Quito and four hundred adults in Guayaquil). But four years later, Durán suffered great loss of popularity after the shock. The determinants of public approval of governments in the wake of policy shifts, and in response to economic reforms, is worthy of research.

41. See Iversen, "The Logics," and Adam Przeworski and John Sprague, *Paper Stones: A History of Electoral Socialism* (Chicago: University of Chicago Press, 1986).

42. The term *technopol* was coined by Richard Feinberg, "Latin America: Back on the Screen," *International Economic Insights* 3, no. 4, 1992, cited in John Williamson, "In Search for a Manual for Technopols," in Williamson, ed., *The Political Economy of Policy Reform* (Washington: Institute for International Economics, 1994), p. 11.

4

Building Citizenship: A Balance Between Solidarity and Responsibility

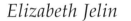

Elizabeth Jelin

To talk about the violation of citizens' rights under dictatorships is easy. But what about in a democracy? Clearly there is a wide gap between the law and its application, and most social struggles are attempts to reduce this gap. There is also a wide gap between the law and the awareness and practice of the rights of the presumed subjects of the law. It is this gap that has provided my interest in investigating citizenship as it is built from the bottom up—that is, through the ways in which people defined as citizens carry out the practices that are concomitant with citizenship. What are the limits and extent of citizenship? In what social relationships does it function? Which institutions must it confront, and in relation to what demands? What is the substance of citizenship?

My purpose here is to analyze the social processes involved in the making of citizenship. One asks how the supposed subjects of the law become citizens through social practices, institutional systems, and cultural representations. The search is aimed at the building of individual and collective subjectivities, both in relation to others in general and to a privileged other, the state or public authority.

The Concept of Citizenship

In democratic theory, the notion of citizenship is grounded in the legal definition of the rights and obligations that go to make it up. The ideological, theoretical, and political debate poses two central issues: the nature of the individual and the content of the individual's

Elizabeth Jelin is senior researcher at the Center for the Study of the State and Society, Buenos Aires.

rights. From a liberal-individualist viewpoint, the former argues for reviewing the citizen's relationship to collective rights; the latter addresses itself to whether universal rights exist and to clarifying the way in which human, civil, political, socioeconomic, and collective rights relate to each other.

These broad questions are still central to the debate and to specific social struggles concerning the formal definition of citizenship (i.e., the establishment of social limits between those who are included and those excluded) and its content (i.e., their rights—the elements on which those who are included can agree).

The widening of the social basis of citizenship (for example, extending the vote to women and to illiterates), the granting of citizenship to minority groups, victims of discrimination, and the dispossessed, and the demand for equality before the law have been continuous issues in contemporary history. The civil rights movement in the United States in the 1960s, the struggle against apartheid in South Africa, feminist demands to halt all forms of discrimination against women, the cry for citizenship among minority ethnic groups—all these are high-profile, international manifestations of the social struggle for inclusion, for equality, and for an end to privilege. There are numerous other instances.

At the same time, there is the debate about the content of equality before the law, about what the state (and, increasingly, the international community) should lay down as guarantees. The broadening of the variety and type of citizens' rights is, in fact, the crux of the social and political history of the last two centuries, first in the West and subsequently in the rest of the world. Once this historical line was broken, according to T. H. Marshall in his book *Citizenship and Social Democracy*, the situation became that which faces us at the end of this century—one of a seemingly chaotic mosaic.[1] After a period of dictatorships in which basic human and political rights were suspended, the transition to democracy is reestablishing political rights. Social rights, however, are in crisis; some civil rights are very much in question. Meanwhile, worldwide concern for the environment, the search for equality before the law, and the recognition of collective rights are crucial issues that put to the proof the very basis of the notion of national sovereignty.[2]

Such ideas, in their turn, indicate a new approach to the subjects of cultural relativism, tolerance, and respect for differences. Important elements of a recent debate cover a spectrum, from radical cultural relativism, in which anything goes, to the search for the biological roots of human behavior, to new forms of ethnocentrism.[3] Also, stemming from another intellectual tradition, Weberian ideas of rationality and the ethics of responsibility come into their own, leaving open the question of the justification of ends and values.[4] The recognition that there are no rational criteria for the choice between alternative values therefore demands a very special search. It has become essential to find a space where, in recognizing the existence of those very beliefs and values, we can also recognize the urgent need for an ethical and political commitment that accords with the central questions of our times. To avoid suffering, to widen the bases of solidarity, to expand the field of public action and responsibility (although, at the same time, promoting tolerance, respecting independence and difference, and giving a voice to outsiders) may have no ultimate, transcendental justification, and in this sense may be fortuitous; but that does make such commitments the less necessary.[5]

The idea of citizenship is a good place to begin to analyze and develop the subject, if and only if the danger of reifying the concept is avoided—of identifying the rights of citizenship with a group of specific practices such as voting in elections, enjoying freedom of speech, or receiving public benefits of one sort or another.

From a broader analytical viewpoint, the concept of citizenship involves a power struggle that reflects the conflict about who may say what; that defines what the common problems are and how they will be addressed.[6] Citizenship and rights are always in the process of creation and change. More than being a list of particular rights, which is changing and historically specific, this view implies that the basic right is "the right to have rights."[7] It also implies thinking of citizens' action in terms of its capacity for perpetuating and expanding itself. Therefore, "the very actions of the citizens are . . . those which tend to maintain, and make it possible to increase, the future exercise of citizenship."[8]

As well as referring to the extent and variety of rights, citizenship includes the citizen's responsibilities and duties, a subject less studied by theoreticians of citizenship. Even Marshall mentions, but then forgets, the duties. Duty and obligation have something imperative and restraining about them, whereas responsibility—as will be seen below—can be broader and go beyond duty. As Arendt (quoted by Young-Bruehl) points out, this dimension of citizenship has its roots in participation in the public sphere:

> The fundamental deprivation of human rights is manifested first and above all in the deprivation of a place in the world [a political sphere] which makes opinions significant, and actions effective. We became aware of the right to have rights and a right to belong to some kind of organized community, only when millions of people emerged who had lost and could not regain these rights because of

> the new global situation. Man, as it turns out, can lose all so-called
> Rights of Man without losing his essential quality as man, his human
> dignity. Only the loss of a polity expels him from humanity.[9]

This definition includes civic commitment centered around active
participation in the public process (the responsibilities of citizenship) as well as symbolic and ethical aspects based on subjective tendencies that confer a sense of identity and belonging to a group, a
sense of community, or that which fosters a consciousness of being
an individual with the right to have rights. The civic dimension of citizenship derives from feelings that link people to a group (contrast-
ing with the apparently more rational elements of the rights of civil
and social citizenship).[10]

It is clear that the two sides of citizenship present intrinsic tensions and ambiguities, with different sociopolitical evolutions. An important point is the degree in which the development of the rights of
social citizenship by means of the welfare state tends to replace the
ideal of the citizen responsible for the reality of the "client," becoming, in effect, a form of boycott of the very development of a full
sense of the citizen as an individual with rights.[11] In this connection,
the breeding of political forms of client relationships and of populism in Latin America is an element of a political culture that hin-
ders the evolution of a culture of citizenship.

In its turn, citizenship in the dual sense of rights and responsibilities enters into conflict with the process of the emergence of autonomous individuals, revealing the intrinsic impossibility of reconciling the ideals of the creation of autonomous individuals with that
of a more just community.[12] This ambiguity is taken up by Reis.

The ideal of the citizen includes an egalitarian and consensual
element, involving civic and collective virtues as well as the duties
and responsibilities of the citizen. It also includes irremediably an element of the assertion of autonomy on the part of each individual
member of the group—an element that may cause conflict before it
establishes unity and understanding.[13]

In the transition to democracy occurring today, as well as in the
centuries-old process of creating individual and collective forms of
citizenship, both aspects of citizenship appear. One is an openly expressed demand for respect and an extension of citizens' rights,
which were repressed and stored up during periods of dictatorship;
the other is a symbolic demand for a sense of belonging, which is
based on collective identity.[14] In the democracies now under construction, the requirement of being governed and represented, on
the one hand, and citizen participation and control of the running

of government, on the other, are often looked on in the short term as incompatible, thus presenting a difficult choice. In fact, the building of democracy requires both. Representative democracies quickly stop being democracies when they do not concern themselves from the outset with creating institutions through which citizen participation and control can function.

Wherein Oppression Was Held to Be Normal

I shall start this section on Latin America's historical reality with a schematic, simple statement: Even when formally defined and agreed rights existed in theory, in everyday life people did not exercise them; they did not demand them, did not act on them, and did not take possession of them. In general, the lower social sectors treated their subordinate position as normal, thereby confirming the view that social hierarchies were in the natural order of things.

This does not mean that Latin America has not had a rich, complex history of popular struggle. It has. This history led to the expansion of citizenship and rights, through peasants' struggles, workers' protests, and other peoples' movements. There was also, though rarely, political mobilization (as in Argentina, on 17 October 1945, when there were demonstrations to secure the release of Colonel Juan Perón; or, more recently, in Brazil, when popular pressure brought about the impeachment of Fernando Collor de Mello), not to mention the revolutions on which the independence of various countries was founded. This history of struggle shows a rich experience of resistance and opposition to oppression—but it took place against a historical and cultural background wherein oppression was regarded as normal, a fact that has come down to the present and is difficult to bring to an end.

These struggles have produced changes in the reality of the ruling classes. They have also brought about a partial transformation of the legal system, with a broadening of citizens' rights. What has been the impact of this history on the cultural representations of domination and subordination? Has there been a change in the relationship between citizenship and the state? Should we continue to regard the state's paternalistic role as a natural institution of rule? Or is the state beginning to be seen as the judge and legitimate guarantor of the resolution (not just the repression) of social conflicts? Is the state an institution that has to answer to the citizenry?

Despite these struggles, the culture of ruler and ruled shows considerable and deep historical continuity. In the absence of a systematic framework of comparative history, let us take some examples, basing our study on two types of evidence: those that refer directly to the "regularizing" of the subordinating relationship and to movements breaking that relationship. These examples indicate the way toward a consciousness of citizenship, and, at the same time, to mechanisms by which this can be achieved. Rather than looking at the legislative processes for creating rights, let us concentrate on the exercise of citizenship as a practice learned by direct participation.

Dilemmas in the Building of Citizenship

How is citizenship learned? In the process, what happens to social and institutional relationships? From the point of view of the education of individual citizens, what we are dealing with is how reciprocal aspirations are learned. What rights do I have? What are my responsibilities? This process implies a dual game in which the individual simultaneously recognizes the responsibilities of others toward him/her (and his/her rights) and learns his/hers toward others. The process not only implies the learning of aspirations and responsible behavior, it also defines the dimensions of individual responsibility.

These processes do not exist in a vacuum but in specific institutional frameworks, which must be constructed or reconstructed during the transition to democracy. Although the whole institutional network is strongly influenced by the type of political regime, there are important variations. The family as an institution of direct socialization is relatively less vulnerable to the pressure and repression of a dictatorship than are schools, and schools possibly less so than the social networks of young people on street corners. The connection among institutional environments is a highly complex mechanism involving contagion and interpenetration, just as there are processes and spheres that govern institutional differentiation. Dictatorial regimes and state terrorism had considerable social penetration, invading everyday, personal surroundings and spaces that in the social imagination do not come into the political sphere (personal address books, for example). They also generated clandestine spaces of resistance and solidarity, which were not self-defined as either public or political. And these spaces became alternative environments for socialization and the learning of behavior patterns, which later became an important part of the reconstruction of a more public series of institutions.

Transition to democracy involves a reconstruction of state institutions and a transformation of the institutions of civil society. It implies the dismantling of antidemocratic forms of exercising power, whether authoritarian, corporative, or based on pure force. It also implies a change in the rules governing the distribution of power, the recognition and enforcement of rights, and the legitimacy of the social participants. In their turn, people have to adopt behavior and beliefs adequate to or coherent with the notion of democracy and learn to function within the new institutional system.[15] Political leaders and ruling classes must renounce arbitrariness and impunity and learn to recognize and take into account the rights and identities of different social participants. The challenge of the present transition lies in the ability to combine formal institutional changes with the creation and expansion of democratic practices and a culture of citizenship. Hence, the practical relevance of the concerns that are stated here.

The Individual and Relationship with Others

Where individual, interpersonal skills are concerned, responsibility toward others is essential to the link between the generations. For survival through early childhood, dependence is necessary and unavoidable. This dependence persists throughout life, as the individual develops self-perception only within the framework of an essential relationship with others. This relationship marks the evolution of adult social and emotional space.[16] Individual evolution is largely a matter of distinguishing oneself from others, of freeing oneself from parental protection, and then of joining groups and institutions in one's social milieu that are run by the exercise of varying degrees of power. By this process, a broader identity is built up, a *we* that generates ties of responsibility toward others who form part of the larger group.

Addressing the question of the function and behavior of individuals entails setting aside the idea of "universal human nature"; it also entails breaking with positive determinist causes that produce such unarguable axioms as "from such-and-such early childhood experiences stem such-and-such emotional behaviors or social adults," or "from such-and-such a social event stems such-and-such an individual reaction." Rather than being a system of uniform patterns or regular types of behavior, the human condition is riddled with strains and stresses.[17] Thus, circumstances and coincidences and different ways of confronting these tensions help us to understand how and why some people, in certain social conditions, take up positions of solidarity with strangers, feel responsible for the fate of others, or are more disposed to care for and help those who are suffering. The question, as Heller pointed out, is: Good persons exist—how are they possible?[18]

When the temptation to establish temporary relationships and direct causes is eliminated, questions take other forms. The basic question is how to define the *we*. What are its limits? Next, what are the moral principles that guide the individual's actions in relation to this *we*? Lastly—part of the process of maturation and learning, that becomes fundamental when we move on to public spaces and macrosocial relationships—how can we appeal to a third party with authority?

Every culture has its own pattern of teaching responsibility to others. The nature of the responsibility, too, varies from culture to culture, as does the definition of morally responsible tasks. Within the Western framework, this theme emerges as a central concern of the social sciences after the World War II, when solving the problems of violence and evil (so as to prevent their recurrence and to establish a firm basis for solidarity and democracy) became a pressing need for committed intellectuals. Nazi brutality and racism led to classic psychosocial research into the authoritarian personality[19] and to experiments that attempted to determine the parameters of conformity and obedience to arbitrary (and immoral) orders.[20] More recently, in addition to the taking up of the question of how genocide and terrorism are possible, a more explicit concern has been to examine positive aspects of human behavior, such as altruism, moral commitment, and solidarity.[21]

A major concern in this work has been that of how the moral conscience develops. A cognitive (and liberal-individual) outlook prevails in this field, underlining an attachment to rules as the fundamental mark of morality and giving rise to measurements and scales of moral evolution. Nevertheless, a knowing, intellectual attachment to universal values—which, for Western males, is the ideal behavior—is only one possible source of moral behavior. Ignoring differences of culture and class, the inclusion of gender differences begins to reveal alternative sources of moral behavior. Gilligan contrasts a male morality of rights with a female morality of responsibility and caring, showing how the two logics are interconnected. To understand how the tension between responsibilities and rights sustains the dialectic of human development is to see the integration of two disparate modes of experience that are in the end connected. Whereas an ethic of justice proceeds from the premise of equality (that everyone should be treated the same) an ethic of caring rests on the premise of nonviolence (that no one should be hurt). In the representation of maturity, both perspectives converge in the realization that just as inequality adversely affects both parties in an unequal relationship, so, too, is violence destructive for everyone involved.[22]

To reveal the origin of responsible and caring behavior toward others as a manifestation of morality is also the object of a study of non-Jews who helped rescue Jews in Nazi Europe.[23] There is no single explanation for altruism and moral courage. Rescuers point the way: they were and are "ordinary" people. Most had done nothing extraordinary before the war, nor have they done much that is extraordinary since. They were not heroes cast in larger-than-life molds. What most distinguished them were their connections with others in relationships of commitment and caring. Their involvements with Jews grew out of the ways in which they ordinarily related to other people—their characteristic ways of feeling; their perceptions of who should be obeyed; the rules and examples of conduct they learned from parents, friends, and religious and political associates; and their routine ways of deciding what was wrong and what was right. They remind us that such courage is not the province of only independent and the intellectually superior thinkers, but is available to all, through the virtues of connectedness, commitment, and the quality of relationships developed in ordinary human interactions.[24]

In more general terms, then, our theme is the effect of social ties and the strength of communal bonds on the conscience of the individual. The basic elements of this morality are responsibility to others and solidarity with those who suffer. Cultural variations of class and gender appear in the specific type of behavior expected in the environment (whether it manifests as more intimate or more public) where this *we* has evolved.

Throughout the process of socialization, the presence of authority is significant. Learning implies rewards from and punishments by a higher authority—in the patriarchal family, the father, followed by the mother; the school authority; the policeman on the street; the deity, and so forth. The evolution of an individual involves mastering ethical principles that lead to the recognition of difference—between, on the one hand, the ethical principles, and, on the other, the authority, which can be legitimate and legal or arbitrary. An independent, moral subjectivity, prepared to defy power when it is arbitrary and illegitimate, implies a strong *I* that has mastered the criteria of moral authority. And this independence, once achieved, is sustained throughout an individual's life by intersubjective reinforcement, through networks, groups, and participatory institutions.

The Social Plane:
The Institutional Context and the Citizen's Responsibility

On the macrosocial plane, this process of the building of rights and responsibilities references the state, made corporate by institutional machinery (e.g., law and welfare institutions). In democratic theory, these institutions receive their power and legitimacy from the fact that they are representative—that is, from the delegation of power that the citizen gives them. That these institutions are efficient repositories of citizens' representation, however, is not assured by any mechanism of formal democracy. In fact, the Latin American state—which is in the hands of the few, and decidedly not for all—has always been and still is remote from its citizens. This implies that recognition of state institutions, and their legitimacy, by citizens—the subjects of rights—is a long, historical process of social struggle, with no guarantee that the outcome will necessarily be happy and harmonious.

The task of transition is, in this sense, arduous. Starting from a state institutional machinery taken over by authoritarian agents, the challenge is to transform these institutions; the institutions have to change masters. At this point, the relationship that the citizen establishes with state institutions becomes crucial. In fact, in contrast to the everyday functioning of stable democracies, whose aspirations are relatively clear and ordered, during periods of transition it is difficult to know from day to day which tasks a given state agency is responsible for and which are citizens' responsibilities. If we depart from the need for a process of democratization of the state, the hard task of demanding, persuading, promoting, and policing this process falls to the makers of civic society, and, at the same time, and in a speculative way, citizenship is learned and built. In periods of democratic construction in Latin America, not only is legitimacy often felt to be unjust and illegal, it is not achieved. Violations of human rights and violence by the state machinery, corruption by public officials, subterfuges by powerful executives to limit the autonomy of legislatures and the judiciary are well known, as are more traditional forms, such as electoral fraud and the buying of positions. They do not disappear with transition to an electoral regime; they can remain and even be reinforced.

Given this primary reality, the building of democratic institutions becomes a challenge to the capacity of citizenship and the organizations of civil society to effect the transformation of state institutions. Thus, the creation of democratic institutional contexts can come about as a result of and, at the same time, a stimulus for the strengthening of a culture of democratic citizenship. But if the task is titanic, what can be done? Where is the will and power to move forward?

In theory, it is a matter for debate whether the notion of public responsibility to others is or is not an essential feature of the concept of citizenship. Setting this theoretical aspect apart, however, the practices of solidarity and responsibility to others are fundamental in periods of transition, inasmuch as they become basic vectors of the transformation of the relationship between the citizen and the state.

What responsibility are we talking about? What practice of solidarity? In the present provisional approach, the question of solidarity is relatively simple: it is a matter of a practice, based on the identification of others who are suffering as "one of us," the logic of which can be analyzed in interpersonal space.[25] (However, for this interpersonal solidarity to spread to the state, something more is needed. Groups and organizations that are prepared to run risks are required, challenging formal obligations and established norms, in function of a sense of very special social responsibility.

The first idea contained in the concept of responsibility (*positional*, in Heller's terms) covers the obligations associated with a position or leadership role. This is a matter of being in charge, of a responsibility to and for, of a formal obligation, of public knowledge (where ignorance cannot be offered as an example). The fulfilling of obligations may not earn prizes or recognition, but not fulfilling them suggests the likelihood of punishment. If public officials of the new democracies were to take on this kind of responsibility, it would be a highly significant achievement. Much remains to be learned, however.

Another type of responsibility is that involving behavior that goes beyond duty and includes that which transgresses it. This concerns situations in which the individual commits (or omits) certain public actions, even when not obliged to do so and when it would have been possible to do nothing. To act or not to act then becomes a choice that must be addressed only in confrontation with one's own conscience. Not to assume this responsibility has no cost, and can be justified by ignorance, or by claiming personal interest. This type of responsibility to others is the basis of caring behavior in everyday life. It becomes politically important when, in periods of repression and change, people and groups are prepared to run enormous risks by challenging established duties and breaking norms for the sake of values or ethical commitments opposed to the powers that be. Given that in the course of these acts a new value or social good (or new demon) may be appearing in the world, the responsibility involved is a very great one. Heller describes these situations as being of "enormous responsibility" and "world-historical responsibility."[26]

Let us take two important examples reported often in the process of democratization: corruption and the violation of human rights. It is not easy for the state (even in a democracy) to look into human rights violations committed by the state machinery. The weight of security organizations and armed forces, strategic calculations, and political commitments force them to do as little as possible about such violations. Individual victims, who under a dictatorship are voiceless, are politically weak. Because of personal suffering and tragedy and the difficulty of charting a regular pattern in a regime of terror, accusation only finds voice when it is adopted by organizations of national and international solidarity, which coordinate and support the denunciation. They publicize the cause and give it legitimacy. At the same time, they question the legitimacy of the state's activities.

How can we move from this game of opposing forces to a change in state institutions and a consciousness of victims' rights? The human rights movement is a paradigm of the crucial role that third parties, giving legitimacy to the demand, assume. This third party has no formal obligation or established role; it involves unified organizations anchored in the social responsibility of its members, who use universal ethical appeals as a resource. They fulfill a dual function: (1) By legitimizing the demand with regard to the state, they promote changes in state practices; (2) They develop a dual didactic of citizenship, which both teaches how rights are demanded and how citizen control over the state machinery is exercised, as they exercise a continuous monitoring of state action in relation to human rights.

In formal terms, the role of a third party—whose task is to legitimize demands, solve conflicts, and impart justice—should be part of the state itself, within its judicial power. While in democratic theory, the autonomy of powers and access to the judicial machinery when rights are violated (even by the state itself) are the guarantee of the existence of full citizenship, the reality is far from this ideal. This is why it is important that instances of civil society exist that carry on the educational task in society (teaching people to appeal to the judicial power), at the same time promoting the democratization of access and the transparency of the judiciary.

Cases of corruption are different. In the majority of them, no direct victims can be identified; nor is solidarity with the sufferer an important motivation for collective action. There are two responsibilites at play here—that of the official who takes (or does not take) charge of his obligation, and the social responsibility fundamentally pertaining to citizen participation in the exercise of control of government action. Often, institutions for the control of such action exist formally; the point at issue is its autonomy in relation to the different state environments—how to integrate them, how to make them function, and what role citizenship plays in this management.

This is a privileged space for the creation of social movements and organizations of civil society—a field and a space that has rarely been studied. In general, anyone who studies social movements places the emphasis on the dynamic of society (collective identities, social conflicts, oppositions) more than on their intermediary function between the practices of citizens and of the state. Social movements always involve a large dosage of solidarity and of responsibility to others. In the transition to democracy, one of their new tasks is to undertake democratization of the state and the building of citizenship.

Notes

This chapter was translated by Norman Thomas di Giovanni and Susan Ashe. It is a shortened version of a paper presented at a seminar on "Human Rights, Justice, and Society" sponsored by the Centro de Estudios de Estado y Sociedad (CEDES), in Buenos Aires, in October 1992. The original work, which was more fully documented, evolved as part of the project entitled "Human Rights and the Consolidation of Democracy: The Trial of Argentina's Armed Forces," developed by CEDES with the support of the John D. and Catherine T. MacArthur Foundation and the Ford Foundation. For Part 2 of the present study, I wish to acknowledge the contribution of the theoretical research and interdisciplinary debate carried out jointly over a period of two years with my colleagues Susana Kaufman and Silvia Rabich. A good deal of what is written here is a product of that ongoing dialogue, rather than of any individual expertise.

1. T. H. Marshall, *Citizenship and Social Democracy* (New York: Doubleday, 1964).

2. Although it is impossible to establish historical, lineal descent in the sphere of international organisms, we can note the following "generations" of rights: the first was human, civil, and political rights; the second was social and economic rights; the third, collective rights; the fourth, peoples' rights.

3. Clifford Geertz, "Distinguished Lecture: Anti Anti-relativism," *American Anthropologist* 86:2 (June 1984); Richard Rorty, "On Ethnocentrism: A Reply to Clifford Geertz," *Michigan Quarterly Review* 25 (1986): 525–534.

4. Rogers Brubaker, *The Limits of Rationality: An Essay on the Social and Moral Thought of Max Weber* (London: George Allen & Unwin, 1984).

5. Jennifer Schirmer, "The Dilemma of Cultural Diversity and Equivalency in Universal Human Rights Standards," in Theodore E. Downing and Gilbert Kushner, eds., *Human Rights and Anthropology* (Cambridge, Mass.: Cultural Survival, 1988); Zygmunt Bauman, *Modernity and the Holocaust* (Oxford: Polity Press and Blackwell Press, 1991); Richard Rorty, *Contingency, Irony, and Solidarity* (Cambridge: Cambridge University Press, 1989); Agnes Heller, *General Ethics* (Oxford: Basil Blackwell, 1990); Emmanuel Levinas, *Ethique et infini* (Paris: Librairie Artheme Fayard, 1982).

6. Herman van Gunsteren, "Notes on a Theory of Citizenship," in Pierre Birnbaum, Jack Lively, and Geraint Parry, eds., *Democracy, Consensus, and Social Contract* (London: Sage, 1978).

7. Hannah Arendt, *The Origins of Totalitarianism* (New York: Harcourt, Brace & World, 1973); Claude Lefort, "Los derechos del hombre y el estado benefactor," *Vuelta* (July 1987).

8. Herman van Gunsteren, "Notes on a Theory," p. 27; Norbert Lechner, "Los derechos humanos como categoría política," in Waldo Ansaldi, ed., *La ética de la democracia* (Buenos Aires: CLACSO, 1986).

9. Hannah Arendt, "The Rights of Man: What Are They?" *Modern Review* 3, 1 (summer 1949), quoted in Elisabeth Young-Bruehl's *Hannah Arendt. For Love of the World* (New Haven: Yale University Press, 1982). In *On Revolution*, Arendt points out the public nature of the notion of liberty in the French Revolution, and in the American Revolution the "public happiness," the right of the citizen to enter the public sphere, to participate in public power. In the course of later history, the "disappearance of the 'taste for political freedom' as the withdrawal of the individual into an 'inward domain of consciousness' where it finds the only 'appropriate region of human liberty'; from this region, as though from a crumbling fortress, the individual, having got the better of the citizen, will then defend himself against a society which in its turn gets 'the better of individuality.'" Hannah Arendt, *On Revolution* (New York: Viking Press, 1965).

10. In ancient Greek cities, civic responsibility was shown by the close, direct commitment on the part of the individual to the community's social and political affairs. George A. Kelly, "Who Needs a Theory of Citizenship?" *Daedalus* 108: 4 (1979). Modern nationalistic movements tried to build civic commitment through identification with the nation state. The historical result was not always successful, and national bigotry, rigidity, and racism were among the results. Kelly, "Who Needs?"; Fabio Wanderley Reis, "Cidadania, estado e mercado. Democracia social e democracia política no processo de transformação capitalista," conference talk, "Modernización económica, democracia política y democracia social" (Mexico City: El Colegio de México, 1990). The present challenge is how to anchor a sense of community and belonging in an ethical principle of equality, in a humane concern for others, in a concern for mutual rights and recognition.

11. Juergen Habermas, *Legitimation Crisis* (Boston: Beacon Press, 1975); Reis, conference talk, "Modernización."

12. Rorty, *Contingency.*

13. Reis, "Modernización," pp. 10–11.

14. The interaction between the demands of citizenship and the requirements for the construction of a new order is analyzed by Lechner, who points out that the demand for community, which the search for a new collective identity implies, is an important element in the challenge that Chilean society is putting before its new democratic state; Norbert Lechner, "Modernización y modernidad: la búsqueda de ciudadanía," conference talk, "Modernización económica, democracia política y democracia social" (Mexico City: El Colegio de México, 1990).

15. Obviously, not everyone will have to learn things that are entirely new: some remember past democratic practices and are ready to return to them. However, Latin American dictatorships have lasted a long time—so long that many young people have never had the chance to exercise the

democratic right to vote or to serve in an elected government or to enjoy the everyday life of a free citizen. Moreover, even in those countries where political democracy formerly functioned, the ethics and culture of democracy were never strong or prevalent. Decades, or even centuries, of arbitrary rule and a cultural pattern of submission in hierarchical interpersonal relationships (such as the family patriarchy and the inferior status of ethnic minorities) have left a legacy that it will not be easy to change quickly.

16. A psychoanalytical hypothesis says that, in our internal world, we are driven by an overriding need for security in order to protect ourselves from devastating primitive anxieties. We search for security in external reality, and, in this dependence, we are vulnerable and submissive, often despite ourselves. Silvia Amati Sas, "Recuperar la verguenza," in Janine Puget and Rene Kaes, eds., *Violencia de estado y psicoanálisis* (Buenos Aires: Paidás-APDH, 1991).

17. Agnes Heller, *General Ethics.*

18. Ibid., p. 8.

19. Theodore Adorno, et al., *The Authoritarian Personality* (New York: Harper and Row, 1950).

20. Solomon Asch, "Effects of Group Pressure upon the Modifications and Distortion of Judgements," in *Groups, Leadership and Men* (US Office of Naval Research, Pittsburgh: Carnegie Press, 1951); Stanley Milgram, *Obedience to Authority* (New York: Harper and Row, 1974).

21. Lawrence Kohlberg, *The Philosophy of Moral Development* (San Francisco: Harper and Row, 1981); Carol Gilligan, *In a Different Voice: Psychological Theory and Women's Development* (Cambridge: Harvard University Press, 1985); Samuel Oliner and Pearl M. Oliner, *The Altruistic Personality* (New York: Free Press, 1988); Herbert Kelman and V. Lee Hamilton, *Crimes of Obedience: Toward a Psychology of Authority and Responsibility* (New Haven: Yale University Press, 1980); Bauman, *Modernity.*

22. Gilligan, *In a Difference Voice,* p. 174.

23. Oliner and Oliner, *Altruistic.*

24. Ibid., pp. 259–260.

25. The possibility of increasing human solidarity is rooted in "the ability to see more and more traditional differences (of tribe, religion, race, customs, and the like) as unimportant when compared with similarities with respect to pain and humiliation—the ability to think of people wildly different from ourselves as included in the range of 'us'." Rorty, *Contingency,* p. 192.

26. Heller, *General Ethics,* pp. 78–80.

PART 3

THE PROBLEMS AND CONSEQUENCES OF ECONOMIC REFORM

5

New Competitive Tigers or Old Populist Nationalisms?

Moisés Naím

In recent years, more frequently than ever, journalists, academics, investors, and governments have all had to revise their view of Latin America's international economic relations. Throughout the region, an initial wave of optimism surged at the rise of democratic regimes and the promise of trade liberalization.

Later, this optimism came under brief but intense threat. What effect on Latin America would there be from the changes that were taking place in the former Soviet Union and in other former Communist countries—democratic government, market reforms, and trade liberalization? In theory, these new aspirants to capitalism turned themselves into powerful magnets for official aid, foreign investment, and international capital from the world's richest countries. All, of course, at the expense of Latin America (the desperate situation of Africa guaranteed that the focus of the industrialized world's decisionmakers, public, private, and multilateral, on the former Communist countries would not be absolute). This concern was short-lived. Nationalist movements and an entanglement of interests, confusions, and problems typical of the transition to democracy and a market economy brought about the eclipse of the new, formidable rivals in the competition for international capital and trade.

In this way, concern about the impact of Eastern European states and former Soviet republics on Latin American prospects in the international economy was replaced by concern about the economic blocs taking shape in Europe and the Far East. Negotiations for a trading partnership between Mexico, Canada, and the United States

Moisés Naím is senior researcher at the Carnegie Endowment for International Peace.

(the future North American Free Trade Agreement, or NAFTA) and the 1990 proposal by US president Bush for an Initiative for the Americas (by which the hemisphere would unite in agreements designed to facilitate trade and private investment) for a time quelled the anxieties brought about by a world of economic blocs that excluded Latin America. The crisis over the European monetary system and the obvious impossibility of NAFTA, or something like it, extending in the near future to the southern hemisphere were other events that obliged Latin Americans yet again to reexamine their views on the continent's economic future vis-à-vis the world.

But the manner and degree by which Latin America places itself in the global economy have been altered by more than the shifts occurring elsewhere. The region itself is changing and, with few exceptions, economic growth has been reestablished, inflation continues to move downward, and structural changes are making many countries more competitive than has been the case in the past. Attitudes that led to huge inflationary public deficits have been replaced by great fiscal caution, and, with varying degrees of success, all governments are trying to establish networks of social protection to lighten the heavy burden experienced by the region's poor. Although installment payments on foreign debt are still significant, they no longer have the intolerable weight they did a few years ago. In fact, the region has very nearly reestablished normal links with the international financial market. Furthermore, in the first few years of the 1990s, Latin America has attracted an extraordinary amount of capital. Direct foreign investment in the form of investment portfolios, new, private international bank loans, and the unprecedented placement of company shares on the New York, European, and Asian stock exchanges have helped to create a substantial flow of capital into the region. In addition, there has been repatriation of portions of the capital that big Latin American savers keep in other countries.

But not all the changes in Latin America are positive. Other events, too, have molded the expectations of the last two or three years: Alberto Fujimori's autocoup in Peru and Jorge Serrano's in Guatemala; the two failed military attempts in Venezuela to unseat the government of Carlos Andrés Pérez and his enforced departure from the government; the trial of Fernando Collor de Mello in Brazil and the fact of few signs of trade liberalization or economic stability in that country; the growing trade balance deficits of Argentina and Mexico; and the victory of the antiprivatization forces in Uruguay's referendum. In the next two years, the majority of Latin American countries have presidential elections scheduled and opposition to new economic programs is gaining popularity in many places. In

the face of profound national political problems, there is deep uncertainty about the future of the region's international economic
relations.

Defining Factors

It may, thus, be useful to set out a less anecdotal view of the factors
that in the next few years will contribute to defining the foreign policies of Latin American countries. Some of the questions posed bear
on the nature of the various domestic policies and the effect these
may have on foreign policy. It is necessary to underscore the importance of not limiting the scope of the analysis to relations between
the different states and their foreign ministries: the priorities, planning, and influence of other players (governmental and nongovernmental multilateral agencies, business conglomerates, and specific
sectors) must also be taken into account. In this way, we may gain a
more realistic idea of the dynamic that shapes the possibilities and
limitations of Latin American nations in their foreign relations.

It is plain enough that the main worry of Latin American governments in the near future will continue to be the need to reconcile
the social, economic, and political tensions arising from the increased importance of the marketplace. That is the heart of economic activity. Fiscal discipline, deregulation of price and trade controls, free exchange, the opening up of foreign investment, and
privatization have quickly broken down the stagnation and inflation
of the 1980s. However, as is well known, these reforms have political
consequences that, in certain cases, could have a negative effect
on domestic reforms and their long-range stability. If this happens,
the effectiveness of the new economic policies will be hindered, creating even more difficulties for the governments that introduce the
reforms.

What is to be hoped for is that, country by country, foreign policies will largely be determined by the capacity to sustain, over a period of time, economic policies of deregulation and growth based on
each country's expansion of international competitiveness, both in
exports and in attracting foreign investment. A country's foreign policy will suffer changes according to the extent to which political pressures force its government greatly to decrease the degree of international expansion of its economic policies. But not only can the
effectiveness of a country's economic and foreign policies suffer.
Under circumstances marked by the impatience and exhaustion of a
population crippled by financial problems, plagued by a lack of basic

public services, and frustrated by corruption and unfulfilled promises, democracy is also constantly threatened and put to the proof. In many Latin American countries, democracy is a fledgling affair, as yet imperfect and in some ways still fairly experimental. This is why, out of the effort to preserve and consolidate democratic regimes, important points for Latin America's foreign relations will also be derived.

The challenge to consolidate economic reforms and at the same time to deepen the processes of democratization is a monumental one. In almost all of Latin America, the task has to be undertaken in difficult conditions. These conditions vary, but, by and large, they stem from four kinds of deficits or basic insufficiencies. Any given government's domestic policy will be greatly influenced by the country's need to tackle these deficits. The four are: (1) the social deficit, (2) the institutional deficit, (3) the democratic deficit, and (4) the investment deficit.

The social deficit. Many years of false economic policies and a series of circumstances, both domestic and foreign, have heaped on the citizens of Latin American countries a great burden of poverty and inequality. To obtain resources and to identify policies and programs aimed at curbing and eventually curing this poverty will continue to be a central domestic aim of all these countries. The need for a more equitable distribution of income will continue to be a constant source of initiatives, projects, and debate. Alleviation of poverty depends on reduction of inflation, the creation of permanent jobs, and reconstruction of public organisms in charge of policies for health, education, housing, and such public services as transportation and security.

The institutional deficit. For several decades, although Latin American states have rapidly increased their sphere of action and influence, their ability to execute public policies has diminished. With rare exceptions, the region's public organisms for years were without the capacity to accomplish their objectives. Some of the factors that have devastated public administration throughout the region have been: congestion; scarcity of qualified personnel; organizational disorder; lack and bad utilization of resources; the takeover of public organisms by labor unions, political parties, and private groups; the sheer number and confusion of objectives; defects in the legal framework by which these organisms' activities are regulated; high turnover of top-level staff; and instability of policy. And, general corruption, of course, is as much a cause as it is a consequence of all the above.

It is clear that the desperate need to carry out more effective social policies and to improve public services will generate strong pressures for increasing the state's institutional capacity. It will not be easy to accomplish, but there are two new forces in favor of a more efficient state. The first is privatization, which frees resources and cuts the demand for money, management, and time on an already overburdened state. The second is the tendency toward democratization, with consequent single-candidate elections and decentralization, which generates incentives in those heading public administration, making them more sensitive to the demands and expectations of the population they serve and on whom they depend for their jobs.

Moreover, the institutional weakness of Latin American states unwittingly contributes to shaping foreign and domestic policies. The need to deal with this weakness will create further demands on those who govern.

The democratic deficit. The spread of democratic regimes in Latin America has had many consequences. In many countries, the combination of democracy with economic liberalization has helped reduce the traditional power and autonomy of the head of state, with consequent expansion in the power and influence of the legislatures, the judiciary, and provincial governorships. In part, this increase has been at the expense of presidents and ministers.

The elimination of state controls on the economy lessened the dependency of the private sector on the government, which, with the deepening of democratic freedoms, increased the independence and the influence of privately run means of communication. This convergence of factors gave the media much more power and transformed them into even more fundamental political players than they had been.

The process of democratization has also acted as a catalyst for two other important tendencies. The first is the increase in *demand* for greater democracy and for more opportunity to participate. Merely to vote in elections for a president or legislators at regular intervals satisfies fewer and fewer of the democratic expectations of Latin America's urban middle classes. The second is deep *dissatisfaction* with the old, traditional politicians and parties. In Latin America, as in other parts of the world, voters—when given the chance—are rejecting known political figures in favor of candidates not closely linked to the usual centers of power. This phenomenon generates a strong tendency to elect governments that have small majorities, no clear mandates, and widely diversified power structures that weaken their ability to enforce policies.

The investment deficit. The countries of Latin America have accumulated huge balances in their domestic investment, both public and private. In particular, the fiscal crisis that Latin America has long been going through and the tendency to channel public funds to help balance the losses of state enterprises (airlines, steel, telephones, petrochemicals, hotels, and so on) have meant that investment in infrastructure has been neglected—to the point of now reaching critical levels. To deal with the region's electrical energy needs alone, it is estimated that at least $20 billion a year is required over the next ten years. Add to this the investment necessary for water, health, housing, education, and transportation, and the sums are beyond the reach of public investment.

The problem is further complicated by the fact that, in the next few years, other countries and regions will be competing as never before to attract, with identical aims, investment from industry, governments, and multilateral financial institutions. In Latin America, the painfully learned lessons of the hyperinflationary consequences of building up large fiscal deficits have generated a new fiscal caution that limits reverting to the option of financing public investment by deficit spending. Moreover, increasing foreign indebtedness for such projects is not feasible. In order to finance their urgent need for infrastructure, Latin American governments have no options but to augment their fiscal income without driving out private investment, to privatize, and to attract foreign capital. The implications of this reality and similar domestic agendas on foreign policy will be considered in the next section.

Ripe for Integration

What consequences do the domestic agendas of Latin American countries have for their foreign relations? Hopefully, the region's international program is going to be significantly influenced by the need to reduce the above-mentioned deficits as quickly and untraumatically as possible. In particular, the economic objectives derived from new economic policies will impose specific priorities on foreign policy. In fact, all the countries of the region are now, and will continue to be in the years to come, dedicated to preventing new competitor nations from capturing traditional markets for their exports and at the same time trying to open new export markets; attracting investors from abroad for buying and operating privatized industries as well as for engaging in activities to encourage hard-currency earnings (exports, tourism, financial services); creating suitable conditions for bringing back such capital that once fled the region in search of economic and legal protection abroad; maximizing access to official sources of funds for development from the more advanced countries and multilateral financial organisms; reducing, within a framework of action that does not threaten previous objectives, the transfer of funds connected with the servicing of foreign debts.

The logical conclusion of this list of objectives is to make economic integration with countries inside and outside Latin America the primary channel of the region's international relations. While economic integration has always had priority in Latin American rhetoric, the lack of progress in this area has been exceeded only by the volume of discussion the subject has elicited. In the past, economic integration implied the adoption of measures often inconsistent with the guiding principles of a country's economic policies. (Examples of this are the reduction of tariffs in a highly protectionist milieu and the promotion of interregional investment in a national context not conducive to foreign investment.) In such cases, integration efforts responded to defensive impulses and were trying, basically, to extend the policy of import replacement and its natural protectionism beyond a country's borders.

Current new circumstances, however, facilitate integration. Implementing the public policy measures needed to put economic integration into practice among two or more countries that have already liberalized their trade, their exchange, and their foreign investment is clearly more sensible now than it was in the past. In many cases, what agreements between governments do is to formalize, and further stimulate, a de facto situation that private industries are already profiting from. The free trade agreement between Venezuela and Colombia is the best example of this.

It should be emphasized that although all the countries of Latin America have based great hopes on free trade treaties with the United States (and will do whatever is necessary to bring about their realization as soon as possible) such agreements will not prove the most immediate source of expanded export markets. At present, the political and institutional obstacles stopping the United States from concluding free trade agreements with Latin American countries other than Mexico (and perhaps Chile) seem almost insuperable. On the other hand, interregional trade, figures for which are, in theory, almost derisory beside the attractiveness that the North American market holds out, is offering exporters a pleasant surprise. Plainly, for a Latin American company setting out in the export world it is cheaper and easier to take its first steps trading with Colombia, Chile, or Venezuela than to try to break into the North American market. This is why, in the foreseeable future, we may look forward to a major expansion of interregional trade, which could reach unprecedented heights.

We must, for example, expect that for the rest of this decade the likelihood is that trade will be more strongly stimulated in any of the South American countries by the eventual liberalization of trade with Brazil than by the signing of a trade agreement with the United States. The same holds for the successful conclusion to the Uruguay Round of GATT in 1994, which will have a more immediate effect on the opening up of new trading opportunities for South American countries than would agreements with the United States.

From 1970 to the present, intraregional trade among Latin American countries and those of the Caribbean has remained at 1 percent of the total of world trade. Clearly, in view of this low figure, an increase seems a real possibility in the 1990s, when Latin America will be greatly motivated to expand exports as permitted. For this to happen, the integrationist dynamic—with its effects on investment and the opening up of new and varied forms of regional interdependence—will have to shape the foreign policy of the countries involved.

The Other Priorities

On the other hand, international priorities of an economic nature that respond to a country's immediate needs will become inextricably mixed up with priorities of another nature. In some instances, these priorities also originate in the countries that adopt them; in others, they are incorporated into the country's foreign policy as a reaction to the pressures or expectations of the international community or of particular countries. Other fields of international action include protection of the environment and its financing, the war against the drug trade, immigration, human rights, participation in conflicts outside Latin America (Argentinian troops were in the Persian Gulf) or in United Nations–sponsored peacekeeping, or even at some future time in a multilateral force for the restitution of democracy in a given country of the region.

Latin America's diversity is brought out in any analysis of the region. To the existing catalog of differences among the various countries (in culture, resources, social structure, political system, economic structure, levels of development, and so on) another will soon have to be added—the ability of a given country to follow through on economic policies over a sustained period so that it may become an efficient competitor in the world economy. This means the skill to attract and hold foreign capital for investment in export industries or in public services formerly in the hands of the state (telephones, water, electricity, ports). Efficiency is the indispensable key to a more competitive economy. Such policies, in turn, are not sustainable unless the state increases its ability to provide people with basic services and to protect groups that are socially and physically more vulnerable from the onslaught of inflation and poverty.

Growing Stratification

Obviously, Latin American countries will not all advance at the same rate. Most likely, the march toward competitiveness will not be continuous. At times, one country or another will fall into stages of stagnation or even regression in its economic, political, and social transformation. In contrast to the 1970s and 1980s, when economic deterioration took place throughout Latin America, the relative sameness in regional performance has come to an end. Possibly, some countries will carry out their competitive entrance into the world economy in a systematic way and will manage to achieve price stability, greater equality, greater efficiency in the public sector, and a bolstering of democracy. Chile is the obvious hope in this regard. Other countries may alternate between periods of openness, with liberalized economies and democratic politics, and periods of state intervention, fiscal laxity, nationalism, and authoritarianism. Each interlude of this type, however short, has a devastating effect on the confidence of investors. It takes time to correct the economic imbalances and new poverty created by such episodes. However, the more international competition there is for capital and markets, the more serious is the danger of such statist or nationalist intervals occurring. In fact, competition is so great that it is not even necessary for instability to affect economic policy for there to be increased difficulties in bringing about successful transformation.

Immediately after President Fujimoro's autocoup in Peru, for example, if international financial support had been reduced, the political and economic effects might have taken several decades to set right—the risk involved in taking part in privatizations would have deterred prospective private investors; the institutional crisis would have limited the government's ability to relieve poverty; the need to confront drug dealers and terrorists would have led to continuous human rights violations; and institutional instability would have persisted. In Venezuela, political instability has driven out investors and increased the cost of the country's international financing, which of course has reduced resources that might otherwise have been allocated for hospitals, schools, and public security.

The point is that we must expect a growing stratification of Latin American countries in terms of the ability to compete internationally. Greater competitiveness will bring greater ability to deal with the four deficits, and certain countries of the region will gradually begin to eclipse those that have not developed the political and institutional ability to compete.

The twenty-first century is likely to open with a Latin America more sharply divided between countries that have learned to operate in the world economy and to benefit from it and those that are victims of a dynamic that submits them to one unpleasant surprise after another. Geography, history, natural resources, and the existing economic structure are factors that can either facilitate or obstruct a country's future. In the final analysis, the ineffable factor that will determine to which category a country belongs is the quality of its political leadership.

Note

This chapter was translated by Norman Thomas di Giovanni and Susan Ashe.

6

Economic Reform and Democratic Viability

Osvaldo Sunkel

The warm wind of democracy currently blowing over Latin America has significant antecedents in the continent's handful of democracies that date back to before World War II and in the democratizing process that later spread to other countries until well into the 1960s. A series of military and authoritarian governments then took over, lasting until the end of the 1970s, when the present phase of democracy opened.

This thumbnail history is relevant. Latin America's switches between democracy and authoritarianism are to a certain extent—and in a complex way—linked to the continent's economic background and development over the last fifty years. This is not to ignore the great differences among Latin American countries and the often crucial incidence of strictly political factors, decisive personalities, the world context, outside military intervention, and other influences—as well as the complex interaction of all these elements.

I think it reasonable to maintain, however—and this is the theme I have undertaken to explore here—that, at least in the medium and long term, favorable economic conditions will contribute to the strengthening of democracy and, conversely, that conditions of economic crisis will impede and hinder it. It seems to me that the present moment, when the resurgence of Latin American democracy is going hand in hand with an acute economic crisis and drastic measures designed to reorganize the economy and the state, is a good time to look into the terms of my proposition. Will democracy survive today's conditions?

Osvaldo Sunkel is former advisor to the director-general of the Economic Commission on Latin America (ECLA) and president of the Center for Development Studies (CINDES), Santiago.

The first democratic wave in the middle of the century was substantially underpinned economically by the relatively successful strategy of integration of the domestic market along with modernization and planned industrialization, all actively based on a broadening of the state's activities, which began during that period. The system had roots in the appropriation by the state of an ever greater part of the income generated by each country's traditional specialized exports. By virtue of increased productivity and concentration, this became the chief sector of the economy able to generate a large taxable surplus. Thus, the state was able to reallocate these new resources with the aim of promoting both industrial and social development.

After general modernization, the sector most strongly promoted was industry, which was the most backward sector. To achieve industrialization, and owing to the underdevelopment of the economy, the state had to support the private sector in a number of ways. The state was obliged to do all of the following: integrate the domestic market by creating infrastructure in energy, transportation, and communications; set up educational programs at all levels; set up institutions to supply middle- and long-term credit; facilitate wider access to basic products, capital goods, and imported technology; establish public industries to produce such fundamentals as energy, steel, and essential chemical products as well as others that private industry was not equipped to deal with.

The state also responded by extending and dividing up public services according to the growing need for education, health, housing, social work, justice, and an infrastructure of services for a rapidly increasing and ever more urban population. By taking on these new economic and social functions, the state, both directly and indirectly, created a large number of jobs for a variety of social sectors.

In this way, a number of social and political coalitions of a multiclass and populist type came into being, in which management, the middle classes, and the organized working classes all took part. There was even some political support for participation by an emerging urban underclass. This was the foundation for the first wave of the democratizing process mentioned above. It took place at a point, between the late 1940s and the mid-1970s, when the economy was expanding successfully and achieving unprecedented average rates of economic growth and improvement in material welfare. In other words, national income increased and was shared more equitably, mainly by means of the state apparatus. In this new setup, everyone gained, although inequalities persisted and in some cases even worsened, essentially because of increased urban poverty.

During the 1960s, however, the state—the generating force behind development—began to face two increasingly conflicting pressures.

One was an unquenchable thirst for funds to continue the program of industrial expansion and infrastructure and, more than anything else, plans for social welfare. The other concerned exports, the main source of fiscal income. These had remained relatively stagnant owing to protectionist policies and technological tendencies, consumption, and pricing in an industrialized economy as well as an increase in the burden of taxation and the absence of policies to stimulate export expansion and diversification.

Once the principal base of the tax revenue system and the taxation rates reached a certain level, incomes stopped rising at the same rate as the growing needs of the public sector. The political and administrative problems of a quick and efficient expansion of a progressive tax system, together with a nonexistent or precarious fiscal system (not to mention the very nature of a heterogeneous economic structure) then led to an accelerating trend toward public-sector deficit. This was translated into even graver inflationary imbalances, which aggravated the social and political tensions resulting from protectionist dislocations.

The persistence of a traditional export sector, an industrialization policy wholly aimed at the domestic market, and a tax structure geared mainly to foreign trade increased Latin America's dependence on other countries and began to put the brakes on economic growth. One of the most serious aspects of this dependency was the growing vulnerability and structural instability of the balance of payments. This increased according to the extent that foreign exchange income stagnated or was reduced even as the demand for imported goods and services increased with the process of industrialization and modernization and the rise of foreign investment and technology. The growing restrictions on the availability of foreign exchange earnings set limits on imports of manufactured goods and therefore on investment and growth, as did wider gaps in the balance of payments and the fiscal budget, all of which accentuated inflationary pressures and sociopolitical problems. This combination of destabilizing factors at the same time produced a need for a further injection of foreign capital. Thanks to increasingly flexible offers by the international private borrowing system dating from the late 1960s, a foreign debt was acquired that began to grow dramatically from that time on.

During the 1960s, the crisis in postwar industrial systems created severe economic problems and instabilities, with grave political and social repercussions that led to a sharpening and a polarization of political tensions. These were exacerbated by the international context, especially the Cuban Revolution and the attempts at reform inspired by the Alliance for Progress. All this served to weaken the democratic process and provoke coups in several countries. In others, however, democracy managed to rise above these difficulties, which is an interesting fact, inasmuch as it discredits the assumed, simplistic link between economic and political crises.

After that period, a series of changes in development policy and strategy were introduced. These ran the gamut from mere changes of emphasis to drastic repositionings, and they can be placed in three general categories. The first comprises those countries that continued the policies they had been following, although with greater emphasis on the increase and diversification of exports. The other two involved far more radical changes.

One, based on a criticism of theories of dependency, followed a distinctly redistributive, statist, socialistic line. Such were the cases of Chile, Peru, Bolivia, and Argentina. The other, completely opposite, took a clearly monetarist, neoliberal path and opened the economy and foreign trade to outside capital and financing, which relegated the state to a subsidiary role and reconfirmed the function of the market and of national and international private enterprise. This latter tendency found its greatest expression in countries like Costa Rica, Colombia, and Venezuela, which managed to maintain their democracy. In Chile, Argentina, and Uruguay, however, the military governments reacted against populist redistributive policies.

New governments—both authoritarian and democratic—could for a while sustain foreign, fiscal, and inflationary instability as well as rising underemployment, social inequality, and fierce political tensions. In part, this was achieved by repression and by weakening the salaried sectors, but largely it was accomplished by the easy availability of international financing, which made it possible to sustain ever greater imbalances and at the same time to maintain growth by running up an exorbitant foreign debt.

Most Latin American countries were thus able to sidestep the need to reverse these imbalances and carry out the structural reforms required in such matters as the reorganization of production, the expansion and diversification of exports, the establishment of a tax system, modern financial systems, and more efficient social policies. Only in a few countries have some of these reforms been partially achieved. Given the exceptional availability of foreign capital over this period, I maintain that Latin America's lost decade was in fact the 1970s and not, as is usually held, the 1980s.

The economic miracle came to an end with the debt crisis of 1982. This brought into the open the mistaken policies of the 1970s, which caused a sharp rise in the macroeconomic imbalance. This, in turn, added considerably to the structural imbalances inherited from the earlier period of expansion. A clear and unavoidable need arose to confront these two unsustainable realities, respectively, by means of policies of profound adjustment and restructuring. I shall return to this.

From 1979 on, military, authoritarian, and dictatorial governments began to fall one after the other. One of the underlying forces behind these changes was undoubtedly the economic crisis, which kept increasing beneath the veil of the foreign debt and burst into view when the veil was torn away in 1982. This gives rise to another interesting point, which is that authoritarianism—contrary to what is usually held—is no guarantee of a government's surviving an economic crisis.

The Demand for Democracy

But there are other important factors to be taken into account. Among them, we should draw attention to the growing demand for democracy that has manifested itself in recent decades. By *demand for democracy* I mean the aspirations and call for greater participation in the spheres of finance (income, consumption, jobs), social activity (education, mobility, organization), politics (elections, decisionmaking, participation), and culture (access to information, the means of communication, and cultural goods and services).

Among the causes leading to this broadening of the demand for democracy we can point to some that are long term and some short term, some of a domestic nature and others of foreign origin. Among the first should be mentioned the great social changes experienced in recent Latin American history: rapid urbanization and industrialization; partial modernization of agriculture; the expansion of the educational system; the real revolution in the information media and mass communications; and the strengthening of civil society by means of constitutions and the spread of a great variety and diversity of social, economic, political, and cultural organizations at all levels, strata, and sectors of society.

Among the most recent factors, the outstanding one is the total collapse and deep repudiation of the brutal dictatorships that held sway throughout Latin America in the 1970s. In the short period between 1979 and 1989, military rulers were forced out of government in ten or so countries, where civilian rule and democratic political regimes were established or reestablished. Even if the depth of this change in terms of real political power and effective social participation remains to be seen, there is no doubt that in many countries the

115

transformation was a powerful stimulant and ended by unleashing a demand for democracy that had been incubated by the structural changes mentioned earlier and that had been reinforced by the grim experience of the dictatorships, which had repressed all democratic endeavors.

Another important and relatively recent factor is the process of maturation, moderation, renovation, and unification that has come over the main political movements and parties—the left included—all inspired by a new sense of realism and pragmatism, which has tended to make up unified blocs that legitimize the democratic game.

All this was doubtless influenced by the defeat of leftist governments, the difficulties of survival under the military regimes, the harsh experience of exile, and the frustrating efforts of the European social democratic and socialist parties to govern, circumscribed as they were in their political options by a recession and the high degree of internationalization of their economies and societies.

The turbulent international context has also affected the Latin American democratization process. Spain and Portugal provided a stimulus and an important model from Southern Europe, whose cultural influence in Latin America is appreciable. The international human rights policy initiated by President Carter and continued by later US administrations—which, despite ambiguity and contradictions, included help wherever possible in setting up democratic regimes—signified an important positive change in the traditional attitude toward Latin American dictatorships on the part of the United States. Europe's social democratic parties, expressing themselves through an international European policy, especially in regard to Latin America, have acted in the same way. More recently, it would be hard to exaggerate the importance—for the left in general and for Latin America in particular—of the spectacular crisis and collapse of Communism in central Europe and the Soviet Union.

Social Polarization

We may conclude, then, that there is a powerful union of social and political experiences and perspectives, both national and international, that favor and strengthen the setting up and consolidation of democratic regimes in Latin America. But there are also great obstacles. Among them is the persistence of antidemocratic cultures, behavior, and institutions, which are characterized by intolerance, paternalism, clientelism, and authoritarianism. There is also an ongoing, though limited, guerrilla warfare in parts of the continent and the dramatic and ever more aggressive problem of the drug trade. These have spread insidiously to several countries and have led to parox-ysms of violence and militarization that are already characteristic of the countries where the two problems have coalesced. All this has re-inforced negative tendencies leading to the formation of democra-tic regimes that are restrictive, elitist, oligarchic, and increasingly supported and infiltrated by the armed forces.

A contributing factor here has been a widespread contemporary phenomenon involving the internationalization and transnational-ization process of the economies and societies of Latin America. There is an ever stronger bond between segments of the upper and middle classes, the local bourgeoisie and technocracy, and the multi-national economic, financial, military, and technological structures and the media around a highly homogeneous and integrated nu-cleus that shares similar lifestyles and strong political and sociocul-tural affinities. This, at the same time, has led to the disintegration and exclusion of much of the rest of the society, restricting it to a na-tional periphery, divided up into activities, regions, and socially sub-ordinated groups, marginalized, backward, isolated, and crushed by poverty.

This social polarization presents the socioeconomic elites with a critical dilemma for the future of democracy. They will contribute to its consolidation to the extent that they are prepared to bring about the economic and political concessions necessary to incorporate popular sectors effectively into the economy and politics and to share in a less unjust form the terrible consequences of the eco-nomic crises and policies necessary to overcome it. The alternative to a broad, integrated social agreement of this type is the creation of a bloc of minority political and economic power around these elites, which would impose the inevitable policies of adjustment and re-structuring upon the popular majorities, with serious risk of a split in the body politic and the threat of a virtual suspension of the demo-cratic game.

The debt crisis and the policies of adjustment and restructuring that followed have taken a sharply contradictory form in many coun-tries. The ruling classes have placed much of the burden of adjust-ment on the working classes and parts of the middle class, preserving at all cost the privileges and interests of the cosmopolitan sectors of the upper classes and international industries and banks. These last rely politically on the support of ideological currents of the neocon-servative right and could once more give in to the temptation of re-verting to antidemocratic practices and to the armed forces in order to guarantee the continuity of the system.

On the other hand, much of the middle class, the working classes, and the underclass have adhered to the ideologies and political currents of the center and left, which in many cases—and in virtue of the process of renovation referred to—are now geared toward social change within the moderate channels established by democratic legitimacy. But if the effects of the economic crisis and the policies of adjustment and restructuring become too drawn out and too intense, it may prove difficult to maintain moderate stances, and positions might become more radicalized.

Despite this potential contradiction, the postdictatorship political situation could favor the emergence of a basic consensus. An important positive factor here is the recent traumatic experience of particularly inhumane brutal military dictatorships. To the extent by which the center-right and managerial sectors show a real will to accept some economic restrictions in order to contribute to the alleviation of poverty and the center-left continues to favor democracy and moderation, thereby controlling its populist leanings, a possibility is opened whereby governability crises will be minimized. Such a case would allow for the pursuing of reforms conducive to the resumption of development. But for this, all political sectors and ruling groups, as well as the population at large, must take note of the extreme gravity of the socioeconomic situation that they have had to face.

As has already been mentioned, the foreign debt crisis and the even deeper development crisis that was present at the end of the 1960s (but that was avoided thanks to the foreign debt of the 1970s) have imposed deep macroeconomic changes and structural readjustments in most countries of Latin America. Facing the need to reverse an external situation that had been characterized up to 1982 by a great excess of imports over exports and by foreign credit over overseas repayments, it was necessary dramatically to reduce imports and increase overseas repayments. This reorientation in the flow of trade and capital demanded—and has as its logical domestic counterpart —the attainment of substantial surpluses in the sphere of domestic savings, both public and private.

In order to produce enough national savings to satisfy the rules laid down by the negotiators of the debt and the international bank of credit, a number of policies of adjustment and economic restructuring were applied, which aimed at basic action in two spheres. On the one hand, the private sector was forced to reduce its consumption and investment by a massive cutback in income. On the other, strict conditions were imposed on the actions of the public sector, which, having been obliged to guarantee foreign commitments, had

118

to support the considerable cost of adjustment. This was why the
state, limited in its many expenses and functions, cut the number of
civil servants and public salaries, reduced social services, eliminated
subsidies, cut back on public investment, and privatized state activities and industries. At the same time, an attempt was made to raise
fiscal income by means of tax reforms that switched priority to indirect over direct taxation. As both objectives are very difficult to manage in the short term, the fiscal imbalance has generated strong inflationary pressures, which have been, and in some cases continue to
be, difficult to control.

On both fronts, private and public, an attempt has been made to
reduce expenses and generate a surplus of domestic savings that
would subsidize overseas repayments. But the recessive character of
the measures has made it difficult to obtain an increase in savings,
and in consequence the bulk of the adjustment has been converted
both into inflation and a reduction in investment that combine
alarmingly to endanger the stability and future capacity for growth.
Moreover, this combination of policies has been carried out with a
violently regressive slant, laying almost all the burden of the adjustment and restructuring on the middle and working classes. These
have seen a rise in unemployment and underemployment and an increase of the underclass; a reduction in incomes and salaries; an increase in taxes; restrictions in the access to, and increases in the cost
of, education, health, housing, and social security—with concurrent
decline in the quality of these services; and, overall, the frustration
of hopes and opportunities for financial and social betterment stimulated by the return to democracy.

Outlook: Cloudy

In these conditions, the outlook for consolidating current and newly
established democratic regimes is clouded, as the recent experience
of sociopolitical tensions and conflicts in several countries shows.
Not only do some of the countries still have to overcome the problem of foreign debt, they also have to face a profound reorganization
of the state and its relations with civil society in order to rearticulate
a dynamic model of accumulation, growth, and development capable
of regenerating a substantial surplus and an expansion that can satisfy urgent social demands. The plan put forward by international
agencies charged with implementing adjustment and restructuring
policies, as well as by the governments of the industrialized countries, the multinational banks, and Latin American multinational

119

managerial-technocratic sectors, is still a neoliberal ideology and program, despite the fact that the plan's social and dynamic limitations are plain and that its political costs have in some cases been unbearable.

Without doubt, the resumption of development requires new dynamic forms of international insertion; increased productivity, efficiency, and competitiveness; growing savings and investment; cutbacks, rationalization, flexibility, and greater efficiency in the state apparatus; the achievement and maintenance of a reasonable degree of equilibrium in macroeconomic balances, and the perfecting of the role of the market and of private, national, and foreign economic agents.

What is crucial is the nature of the economic policies and political action by which the reforms are carried out. The survival of democratization processes, in my opinion, needs profoundly pragmatic political and economic programs that take these new realities and requirements into account and are able to bring together wide social sectors and movements that make it possible to deal with the enormous challenge of reconciling essential reforms with certain conditions necessary for recovering the development process. Among other basic requirements, there is the immediate need to improve at least the living standards of those sectors that suffered most deterioration during the past decades and that are most vulnerable to the policies of adjustment and restructuring; to achieve an increase and diversification in exports by a rise in productivity and other deliberate policies—and not only by the indiscriminate reduction of customs duties and the lowering of salaries; to adopt concrete means and practices for regional cooperation and integration and foreign negotiation over the matters of debt, access to markets, and financing; to assure that the decentralization and privatization of public services and industries are carried out openly and in a way that stimulates civil society, improves social and political participation, and strengthens large, medium, and small private as well as cooperative industry; and—given the necessary reorganization—to boost the basic public functions of the state and its capacity to guide economic development, especially in social and environmental matters and in its control of public, private, national, and foreign monopolies.

In short, the main economic focus ought to be revised in the light of these and other considerations and made flexible through political plans and creative economics in terms of the foreign debt, reform of the state, social policies, international reinsertion, productive restructuring, and technical accumulation and progress—all of which will make it possible to sustain both the economic reorganization and the process of democratization, which is now under such threat. Economic conditions cannot make up a rigid, dogmatic framework, but they impose limits whose width or narrowness depend on the efficiency, creativity, and responsibility with which the political actors and technical teams (including those of the international financial agencies) manage to articulate and lead the political process and economic reform. The challenge is formidable, but so is the opportunity to reorganize Latin American economies and societies so that they may reach a new stage of sustainable democratic development.

In any case, while we cannot claim that history shows that democracy founders in the face of crisis and economic reorganization, its consolidation requires proposals that rise above the neoliberal and neoconservative ideologies currently in vogue in Latin America, both in the economic and political spheres.[1]

It is fundamental to recognize that economic reform has been imposed in response to profound objective reasons and domestic realities, as well as for reasons emanating from international structural changes, in particular, the advanced process of the multinationalization and globalization of economies and culture. As such, economic reform is necessary and inevitable. This would have been the case even without the predominance of neoconservative and neoliberal ideology or the collapse of Soviet Socialism.

Therefore, what we have known up to now as economic reform is only one of several possible alternatives—the neoliberal. This is a uniform prescription that pursues the objectives of a reduction of the role of the state; economic privatization, deregulation, and liberalization; and confidence in the market and private industry.

Effects of Neoliberalism

To agree on these general objectives, which have been imposed by the force of new domestic and foreign realities, does not, however, necessarily imply agreement with the means, instruments, and methods needed to attain such objectives. Those currently imposing neoliberal economic reform—and worse, superimposing themselves on the development and debt crises—are having devastating effects on the economy and social system. There has been a low investment, a rapid technological obsolescence and stagnation, a sharp deterioration of the infrastructure, high unemployment, a dramatic lowering of salaries, a violent reduction of social expenditure, a severe deterioration of public services (i.e., education, health, housing, and social security) massive increases in marginality and malnutrition, and with all this the revival and intensification of the deadly cycle of violence, delinquency, and repression.

Inequality has sharply increased, especially because at the other extreme of the social spectrum a small, extremely privileged and favored group has emerged as a result of neoliberal economic reform, giving rise to a new concentration of wealth, incomes, and power. Undoubtedly, one of the first consequences of this socioeconomic polarization is the beginning of the erosion of democracy. In my view, this is the cycle that Latin American countries are presently going through, each with its own level of intensity and degrees of decline, stagnation, or achievement.

The worst phase seems to have been overcome, and in certain Latin American countries economic growth has been reestablished. This is the case in Chile, which has come out of a purgatory of about fifteen years, and in Brazil and Costa Rica. At the other extreme are Ecuador and, surprisingly, Colombia, which in view of their previous reasonable progress—quite different from the rest of Latin America—seemed only to require minor adjustments. But recently these countries have embarked on drastic, unexpected processes of reform. It is to be hoped that the enormous, costly errors made by the countries that preceded Ecuador and Columbia will not be repeated. Peru is in decline, as is Mexico, with its cycles of progress and decline. Bolivia has stabilized but not fully recovered from structural adjustment, and Argentina has not yet consolidated itself.

I suggest that we must recognize once and for all that, for all social sectors and participants, the passage through purgatory to economic reform is as inevitable as it is necessary. The social costs are enormous but limited in time if the reform is carried out as soon and as successfully as possible, for the sooner growth is resumed the more possible will it be to reverse any tendency to social and political decline.

Worse will ensue, the purgatory will persist if the reform is postponed indefinitely, if it is only halfhearted or made without conviction and achieves no success. A hospital patient in need of surgery can remain in surgery, barely survive, or recover fully. What is inevitable is the surgery—economic reform. Without economic reform there is no chance of recovery. What can, to some degree, be avoided is the extent and duration of the social cost. There is also the possibility that the chance of survival, recovery, and growth can be increased. But economic reform is inevitable and necessary. What is not inevitable or necessary is an ultra-neoliberal economic reform, as in the policies of Thatcher, Reagan, and the Chilean Chicago Boys, with its serious economic and social costs.

As I pointed out earlier, there are more moderate and less expensive ways of applying the economic policy measures needed to carry out reform. Their use depends on the following basic factors:

1. The capacity of the political system to recognize its own predicament, renew itself radically, and understand that economic reform is a contemporary historical necessity, and—based on this recognition—to design, structure, and maintain a broad social and political agreement toward a more equal distribution of the inevitable social costs and subsequent benefits of adjustment and restructuring.
2. The capacity of technical teams to collaborate in sociopolitical negotiation, modifying the standard technocratic neoliberal prescription and designing and achieving a group of democratically agreed-upon policies for economic reform that pursue similar objectives but have less recessive effects, are more gradual and moderate, less unilateral, and more balanced, and have a greater concern for attenuating and better distributing social costs and achieving a speedy reactivation and more equal growth in the middle and long term.
3. The capacity for mutual support, cooperation, integration, and solidarity on political, cultural, economic, and social planes among the Latin American countries, emphasizing above all the completion of specific projects and practices among actual relevant participants, especially favoring rapprochement with those countries that are relatively more advanced and committed to the process of economic reform.
4. The capacity for collaboration by the developed countries, radically to improve the international context through their economic growth, the opening up of their foreign trade, and increase in finance and investment in Latin America (so that the region's net flow becomes positive and grows rapidly), and increased international cooperation, principally to facilitate the transfer of technology.

How can these factors be put in place? In the end, most of it depends on us—on our collective, national, Latin American readiness to recognize the originality, the newness, the seriousness, and the importance of the crisis and to understand the need for a profound transformation of our institutions, relations, and political and economic behavior, both national and international; and on whether we will manage to reconstruct a new social pact, adequate to current domestic and international conditions. If we are not in democratic agreement, consensus, and cooperation, economic reform of some kind will be imposed on us anyhow, and its costs will tend to be extremely high, involving great risk to the preservation and deepening of democracy.

For economic reform to succeed in such a way as to set the countries of Latin America on the path to a dynamic and equitable development, both politics and economics will have to function within a democratic framework.

Notes

This chapter was translated by Norman Thomas di Giovanni and Susan Ashe.

1. There is a large literature on this subject. See, among others, CEPAL (Economic Commission for Latin America), *Transformación productiva con equidad* (Santiago: 1990); CEPAL, Equidad social y transformación productiva, un enfoque integrado (Santiago: 1992); O. Sunkel, ed., "El desarrollo desde dentro; un enfoque neoestructuralista para América Latina," Fondo de Cultura Económica, México, 1991; O. Sunkel and G. Zuleta, "La política de desarrollo en la encrucijada de los noventa: neoliberalismo versus neo-estructuralismo," *Revista de la CEPAL,* no. 42, December 1990.

PART 4

LATIN AMERICAN DEMOCRACIES IN THE NEW WORLD ORDER

7

Changing Paradigms in Latin America: From Dependency to Neoliberalism in the International Context

Juan Gabriel Valdes

It is a truism that the vast tide of change that has overtaken the world in recent years has occurred in places a long way from Latin America. This does not mean, however, that Latin America has been unaware of these changes, that the region has not felt them, or that they have had no impact on its people. Carlos Fuentes remarked not long ago that there are years when nothing happens and others in which centuries unfold. Oddly, while no one disputes that in the world's case the last few years have seemed centuries, there are many who take the view that in this same period little has transpired in Latin America. I find this outlook particularly apparent in European newspaper coverage of events in that part of the world, and I wonder whether such a state of affairs has anything to do with the attitude of a former United States secretary of state, who said that he did not mind what decision was made about Latin America so long as he did not have to think about it.

The Europe of this past decade, unlike that of the one before, is not finding it easy to work up an interest in Latin America. It is hard, in fact, to find a viewpoint in Europe today that makes any attempt to recognize the signs of change that are under way in the region; instead, Latin America is looked on as a kind of a lesson that, once grasped, is thought to be forever unchangeable. Of course, events in what used to be the Soviet Union and the collapse of Communism have been too important historically not to have drawn the whole world's attention. But we must also remember that it is not long since Latin America was the land of great ideological adventure for

Juan Gabriel Valdes is former Chilean ambassador to Spain and senior researcher for the Center for Transnational Studies, Santiago.

both the extreme right and the extreme left. These concerns, which stirred the hearts and minds of many European intellectuals, gave rise to a great deal of theorizing about what was good for others, some of which Latin Americans tried out and at times suffered for. European concern later accounted for great movements of democratic solidarity against Latin American dictatorships. Such solidarity, for which the people of Latin America will always have reason to be profoundly grateful, kept democratic ideals and human rights alive and helped save many lives. European support also hastened the return to a state of freedom. But what has happened subsequently is that today, while the proximity of those times serves to remind Latin Americans of dangers to avoid, Europeans look back on that tragic period with an unwitting nostalgia. We all know that the press seldom prints good news, but what galls Latin Americans is that in Europe—especially in Spain—good news from our part of the world upsets the commonly held notions of a whole generation accustomed only to a Latin America with which Europeans can show solidarity. They are only interested in Latin America insofar as it moves them, a recipe that requires a tragedy, a military coup, or a glimpse of the poverty that, to our shame, is so widespread on our continent. The fact of the matter is that in the eyes of many Europeans, we Latin Americans do not exist without such ingredients.

Perhaps our burgeoning literature is to blame for having unconsciously encouraged readers to want Latin American reality to go on accommodating a mythic world of tyrants and heroes and politics that, unlike other contemporary politics, does not fall into a sterile setting of macroeconomic data and predictable, innocuous periodic elections. There is no doubt that Latin America produces less news than before. Nowadays, with all the elections, privatizations, and commercial activity, only Fidel Castro, and to some degree President Fujimori of Peru, live up to European expectations of the good old Latin American authoritarian tradition. The region, however, has entered a distinct new phase and finds itself facing great opportunities and dangers that are quite different from those of the past. Alongside the restoration of democracy throughout most of the continent, Latin America is quietly undergoing change that—with certain obvious differences—holds for the region a significance comparable to that currently felt in Eastern Europe or that which Southeast Asia experienced a few decades ago. This is a transformation that seems in principle to encapsulate its own definition of itself—that is, the way that Latin Americans perceive their part of the world and reflect on its development. What is at issue here is whether this new phase, thrust as it is into dizzying global change, can instigate a leap toward development in the region or whether it will become a new source of frustration and radical action. For the moment, there is no way of telling.

The transformation I would like to take up here has a wider scope and origin insofar as it covers the ideas and conceptions that Latin Americans have of themselves. For this reason, I want to focus my remarks on change in the ideological paradigm and in the perceptions that Latin Americans are nourished on with regard to their inclusion in the international system. Here too, of course, the earlier question is pertinent. Are the new tendencies to be seen in the Latin American debate on development simply short-term ideological phenomena, positive reactions to fashionable tendencies in the developed world? Or is a new mentality being created, the product of profound international change and of the lessons of two decades of violence, dictatorship, and frustration?

Whatever the answer, there is no doubt that Latin Americans are face to face with a new political paradigm. By *new* I do not mean to imply that it is novel. Like the ideas that are being replaced, the new ones are rooted in Western political and economic thought. In this sense, these "new" ideas are the product of North American influence in the region and they express the resurgence of human rights and the optimism about democratic values dating from the beginning of the *anno mirabilis* 1989 as well as the neoliberal expansion that governed economic thought in the 1970s and 1980s. At the same time, it is undeniable that this paradigm, which is not the same throughout Latin America, varies substantially from country to country. However, it does seem clear that the paradigm is predominant among the elite of the region's major countries. The topic of conversation is always the same—the conditions for promoting Latin American development.

Right now, however, the central point seems to revolve about the definition of national interests, which include competitive incorporation into foreign markets, and modernization, which incorporates democracy, and the struggle against problems of social marginalization. This is a national debate inasmuch as its principal elements— democracy, the market, integration, and modernization—seem in all these countries to be included in the aims of the left, the center, and the right. The enemies in this new debate are protectionism, populist tendencies (which are said to produce inflation), authoritarianism, and militarism. The debate, which calls for a moderate Latin American participation in international affairs and negotiation rather than confrontation, is beginning to find in the region's so-called integrationist initiative greater political and economic purpose. In this way, it seems to be rejecting the idea of an abandoned, neglected, marginalized Latin America, a passive object able only to suffer the impact of the international system.

This notion—the natural counterpart of Europe's view in the 1960s and 1970s of a colonized, revolutionary Latin America—always had the significant effect of playing down the responsibility of Latin Americans themselves in the unfolding of national crises and of somehow blaming them on overseas factors, which had to be over-ridden by a complete rupture with the industrial nations responsible for them. In this area, there has been substantial change—but not because overseas factors that dominate, limit, or even destabilize national arrangements are being ignored or because these factors have suddenly grown weak. No one denies that colonization and dependency have been determinants in the historical development of Latin America and that in large measure they continue to be. The difference is that today, behind the changes that have taken place in the international system, the perception of development no longer stops at any secret or explicit desire to eliminate the factor of external power—a desire variously expressed as the "leap outside capitalism," or magic and tragic "liberation," or an idealistic search for a "third way." After the end of a polarized world, such options are both absurd and impossible. The idea of revolution ceases to make sense, and another prospect for change and national integration has arisen. What heartens the region's elite leaders is the belief that they have found the national interest. This interest will be achieved by the integration of a competitive economy in the international marketplace, will be empowered by centrist politics, and will find in the search for social consensus the best path toward social integration.

This, then, is the view that seems to have replaced any desire for revolution or for protectionism (economic, political, and cultural) from the intervention (ownership or active presence) of so-called imperialist centers. What this view represents is another *mentalitä*, to employ the term used by the French for that state of ideas that are more solid than those that predominated from the 1930s to the 1960s and 1970s in fragile, transient ideologies. Nowadays, the issue of combating the social conditions that keep the greater part of the population of Latin America living a marginal existence has been taken out of the context of conflict and is being re-thought as part and parcel of the program of modernization. The cure for marginalization is no longer looked for in revenge by indigenous peoples for centuries-old wrongs or by workers on their exploiters. The only cure will be found in economic growth, job creation, and an improvement in the quality of education.

Similarly, the old paradigm of dependence, once so important to Latin American political and social thought, has been replaced by one of modernization, which means an increase in competitiveness in a world whose wealth, in fact, consists of interdependency. Herein arises a new perspective on the conflict between poor and rich countries, which is mainly the latter's protectionism, but this is a different conflict from the anti-imperialist, structural one expressed by the polarized world and that marked Latin American resistance to capitalist economies, beginning with that of North America.

In short, with the progressive definition and acceptance of the new paradigm by the Latin American elite, corporatist, protectionist, and statist points of view—once the backbone of both right- and left-wing thought—also melt away. For decades, protectionism and statism were two sides of the same coin of the accommodation between the property-owning classes and a state that sought, by an outward appearance of democracy, to bring the lower classes into the system. As everyone knows, the scheme's forward thrust was provided by populism, with the brake on it applied by military coups. The whole cycle was oiled by an ideology of hemispheric security that could invest potential conflict with the threat of Communist infiltration. The elements of this equation no longer exist. If the integration of the global economy renders unviable any development based on state economic controls, the collapse of Communism weakens both radical alternatives and the ideology of national security, offering the several Latin American states greater autonomy to choose new modes of change. The situation has changed, then, because the visionary nature of development plans is not the same today, either for those who set a premium on social integration, whom we can still call the left, or those who pursue economic growth, whom we may define as the right. The two viewpoints are mutually contradictory or complimentary to an introduction of the respective economies and societies into a system that everyone regards as modern.

Is this, then, a case of a new mentality or of a passing ideological wave? I do not think it really possible at this point to give a categorical answer. But it can be safely stated that, barring a sudden change in the politics of the developed countries, the tendency of the main Latin American countries will continue for the rest of this century along the lines just given. In any case, its seems quite unlikely that there will be a return to what was described in the earlier paradigm. If so, a more relevant question may be asked. Is it possible to solve the problems that beset so many Latin American countries—acute poverty, growing disparity in the distribution of income, poor education and health care, social integration—by means of incorporation into the world economy? I am tempted to reply that, in principle, a simple change of paradigm is not enough. In fact, once the sudden change of paradigm and its ever more general and shared character are recognized, it must be remarked that the change described is no more (or less) than the necessary and indispensible accommodation of Latin America into existing international conditions. Also, that even if this accommodation brings us back from the abyss and takes us—if I may mix the metaphor—to the surface of the earth, there is no guarantee whatever that we shall now be able to run.

In short, what has been established after a period of paralysis, authoritarianism, and economic decline is a scenario conducive to an attempt to integrate into world markets. Each country starts from a different point and under widely differing circumstances. Meanwhile, the results of the rash attempt remain to be seen. But it is encouraging to find that some countries have set out with success and satisfaction.

To evaluate this success, it must first be pointed out that the main pitfalls in the road ahead are to be found in the paradigm's very framework. Foremost among these is the discrediting of state action, the weakening of its capacity to act, which runs all the way from the ideological aspiration for an ideologically defective state to the discrediting of the political will as an element of violation in the free play of the market. The establishment of a market economy different from the previous one could make us repeat the phenomenon of ideological fundamentalism so typical of the region—this time by the frenetic adoption of a market ideology that disregards the new fundamental role that the state should play in social development. The second point in an evaluation of the new model's real chances of success is related to the political will and to the capacity for negotiation that that will is able to build up in the management of hemispheric relations, especially in the efforts toward a coordination of Latin American economies and politics. I will remark briefly on these two subjects.

The Social Consequences of Antistate Radicalism

The past few years are often looked on as an expression of the victory of Frederick von Hayek, the Austrian-born economist, over Karl Marx. In their euphoria, however, neoliberals forget that one of the century's most mistaken predictions was Hayek's claim—made in his 1944 best-selling study *The Road to Serfdom*—that state intervention in the economies of European countries would lead to a totalitarian control of life. In point of fact, it is social democracy that has given Europe the highest levels of freedom, welfare, and development ever known in the Western world. Nor does the present crisis in the welfare state fulfil Hayek's forecast. Pressure to reduce the size of the state, to increase its efficiency, and to coordinate its social tasks with the dynamics of production do not justify the wave of antistate ideology disseminated by Margaret Thatcher, Ronald Reagan, and other contemporary purveyors of the Austrian professor's ideas.

Somehow the change in the Latin American paradigm is also the result of the crisis in that form of welfare state known as "the compromise state." From the 1930s on, this model managed to combine a moderate rate of growth with a modest—and in most of Latin America, a fairly precarious—level of democracy. The model was based on a concept of national development geared to domestic markets and on a plan of import substitution in which the state played a dominant role, while the subordinate, weaker private sector asked for and received tariff protection against foreign competition. On the political side, the compromise state regulated social conflict and set up fragile agreements among the groups incorporated into the system as well as between them and the lower social classes. The model went into crisis in the 1960s and 1970s, and this particular type of capitalism in Latin America is now played out.

It is worth emphasizing the capitalist element here, because one aspect of neoliberal ideology has been the rewriting of the recent past to portray the compromise state as socialist. Clearly, with the exception of Cuba, Latin America, even in its most statist and protectionist periods, never organized its economies on any but capitalist lines. Diminished and regulated as it was, the marketplace always held sway. The private sector, receiving the state protection it desired, was always an essential economic (and political) factor. Import substitution ended not because it was socialist but because it was geared to a brand of capitalism that was unable to function in the international style of trading that began to be imposed on the world economy. In each country, the policy was marked by an inability to combine moderate economic growth with even a timid inclusion into the system of social groups that had been marginal for decades, if not centuries. Thus was import substitution perceived by the left, which pursued statism relentlessly, intending "to leap outside the system" either by guerrilla tactics or by large labor parties, and by internal financial power groups, the great multinationals, and the international financial system, which, dismissing the policy as interventionist and redistributionist, fought it as an obstacle to internationalization. This was why in many Latin American countries the end of the development model led to the end of the democratic process and the enthronement of military dictators.

Then, as often happens in structural crises, the performers who have managed to make their mark redraw the picture of what was there before, turning it into something intolerable. The present demonization of import substitution and of the compromise state hides the fact that the latter, in its almost forty years of existence in Latin America, notched up several successes in the field of economic growth and social development. Taking into account the differences between the various countries, the development model led to noteworthy advances in education, health, and the general improvement in conditions for a vast social stratum. However, it is more important to emphasize that from the end of the 1970s and 1980s, the gravity of the crisis promoted an inevitable modification in the model's basic premises. In a little more than a decade, marked in some places by dictatorships and in others by the inauguration of democratic regimes, Latin America underwent a major transformation in its forms of economic organization, and the central tenets of the import-substitution/industrial development model were scrapped. Foreign development was pursued instead of domestic, a policy that opened up the various economies and turned them toward exports. Instead of the state as leader and producer, there was a shift to a powerful private sector and a reduction of state power. The emphasis on national integration and social development was replaced by the imperative for economic growth. Economics displaced sociology as the principal social science.

By now these tendencies have been forcefully expressed. The opening up of the economies and the privatization process, first in Chile and then in other countries—Argentina, Mexico, Peru, Bolivia—are clearly on the rise. The new phase seems to have acquired a dynamic that boosts growth, generates specialization of the apparatus of production in certain exports, and forms a distinctive and more up-to-date entrepreneurial class, whose sights are set on foreign competition. In the framework of the return by many Latin American countries to democratic politics, the ideology of the functioning of the market mechanism and the power of exports is seen as clothed in the legitimacy of a national plan. The idea of "opening markets for our products," of "empowering our workers," and of "adding technology to our natural resources" endows the new phase with a particular epic dimension and greatly modifies the self-perception of the performers and of their countries, just as it does the form as understood by public function and social activity in general.

In short, after a lost decade a new concept of Latin America and its development—marked by profound change in the organization of the region's economies—gives a boost to development and allows hopes to be nurtured for its consolidation in various countries of the area. It remains to be seen, however, how in its new role the state can deal with the task of eradicating poverty and imposing the social conditions that make economic growth compatible with the democracies. This is where the main question arises and where some of the ideological elements of the new model become clearly dysfunctional.

In Latin America, as in Europe, the change of paradigm is often looked on as dominated by an ideology in tune with market extremism. In my view, the spread of antistate radicalism hides a deep insensitivity to the social consequences of the processes of adjustment and economic reorganization. The diminishing of the state's role in the field of poverty assistance, education, and health only increases social marginality, which makes it very hard for democratic regimes to operate. Nevertheless, it is not unusual today to listen to an economic debate that predicates the extension of market rules to the regulation of social relations and that sometimes even declares, as a positive goal, the disappearance of politics. As I see it, this ideology may paradoxically become a threat to the new paradigm that, in so many senses, it resembles.

The social legitimization of the new functions of the private sector demands that privatization not be seen by society as the theft of public property by oligarchies; that, equally, export activity is constituted into a national activity; and that the private sector is incorporated into the task of developing and integrating society. In short, what is required is that the modernization of the economy and of society be made legitimate. To this end, neoliberalism and its derogatory view of the state's role in social assistance and development will quite obviously make no contribution.

The new paradigm of Latin American development, then, requires a new dynamic state capable of enforcing the national interest. Only with a balance and complement between the functions of the public and private sectors, between the state and the marketplace, between politics and the administration of the economy, will the paradigm of modernization become a stage from which development can be given a decisive thrust.

On Integration

In integrating into open multilateral trade, care must be taken to diversify markets and to take advantage of the nearest and most favorable resulting spaces. The change of paradigm and ensuing changes in the international system do not mean a renunciation of the coordination and integration of trade within Latin America—quite the contrary. Latin America today is finding more favorable international conditions—together with more autonomy—than during the cold war. The first of these conditions is a positive change in relations with the United States. This change must be used to advantage, however, and not imply any neglect of the main consideration, which is Latin American economic and commercial cooperation. The point is worth emphasizing, because the change of paradigm has been accompanied by a debate whose anti-integrationist tendency is another great pitfall in the consolidation and success of the new scheme.

We know why in Latin America the collapse of the Communist regimes of Eastern Europe and the newfound cooperation between the United States and Russia has had an impact both on our view of the United States and on the doctrines of national security that did so much damage to our democratic processes. Certain elements of tension in our relations with the United States very quickly disappeared. Some are obvious. Nothing, or almost nothing, and no one, or almost no one, could today be challenged by Washington as being pro-Soviet. The charge of being soft on Communism, which for decades faced so many Latin American projects and so many of its leaders, has vanished. The cold war, in fact, had promoted throughout the region a perverse tension between continental security and social and economic crisis. The significance that certain elements of Latin America's ruling elite drew from North America's overriding interest in security was that any attempt at social change (matters as central and as various as public education, the fight against poverty, the role of the state in the economy, and the alignment of foreign trade) was open to accusations of undermining the continent's security. Security came to determine the makeup and outlook of such key groups as the armed forces. Each conflict over the economic orientation of Latin American countries was transformed and often radicalized into a zero-sum game, which implied staying in or leaving (or being excluded from) what was known as the Western world.

Yet within the framework established by the post–cold war period, the problem of security has tended to diminish drastically in importance as new subjects have arisen to define US–Latin American relations. In the main, these have been trade, immigration, and drugs, and out of them come Latin America's new importance to the United States. With regard to trade, for example, during 1992—in the midst of a recession—US exports to nonindustrialized countries grew by 15 percent, which meant the creation of 400,000 jobs. North American exports to Mexico have tripled since 1986; those to Chile have doubled since 1988. As for immigration, the influx of Mexicans and Central Americans into the United States is well known. In fact, about 10 percent of the population of Central America emigrated to the United States during the civil wars that ravaged those countries in the 1980s, and today the United States boasts a population of twenty million Latinos. With drugs, to enter into negative terrain, Latin America produces 80 percent of the cocaine and marijuana that flows through or is used in the United States (relations between the two continents are not entirely one-sided). President Bush's proposal, in 1990, to move toward free trade in the hemisphere was rapidly taken on board by the various Latin American governments, but it has not yet been translated into anything concrete beyond the consummation of the North American Free Trade Agreement with Mexico and Canada in 1993, promises to Chile that it will be added in 1995, and vague promises to all the other nations at the summit in Miami in December 1994 that there would soon be a hemispheric free trade area.

The importance of the opening up of North American markets to Latin American goods is self-evident. So is the relevance that US investment takes on for open economies like those of present-day Latin America. It should be noted, however, that if over the next few years the main thrust of many Latin American economies is centered on a diversification of markets and on an increase in the proportion of manufactured goods in their foreign exports, the issue of the integration of the region's markets with the US market will have to be carefully revised. What may be suitable for Mexico, which has a common frontier and an economy closely linked to that of the United States, may not so be for other Latin American countries. Equally, the fact that the United States finds in Latin America today the goodwill and genuine interest to widen relations in all fields, the basis for which has not before existed since Latin America won its independence from Spain early in the last century, amounts to a favorable climate for widening ties, but this in no way means that the two parties share identical interests. It remains to be seen whether Washington even understands the extent of the opportunity it has in Latin America.

Every time Latin America enters a period of optimism and consensus about what model to follow, the issue of integration becomes a top priority and leads to new frustration. Rarely, however, have conditions been more favorable than the present as regards the political will. The region has democratic governments almost everywhere. These regimes have similar economic systems and find themselves (albeit at different stages) along the same road of opening up their economies, of privatization, and of strengthening export sectors. A

137

proposal, then, to further the processes of economic coordination and complementarity seems eminently feasible.

Joint work in the Rio Group has proved the optimism well founded. In contrast to other periods, when the subject of integration was taken up in a context of ideological fervor and linked to a debate about the historical imperative for a great Latin American undertaking, the rhythm of the coordination today is slower—less high-sounding. Perhaps this is part and parcel of the region's greater recognition of the deep differences that exist between countries. Thus, the Chilean-based Economic Commission for Latin America and the Caribbean recently indicated that the four principal Latin American economies accounted for 75 percent of the region's gross national product (GNP) in 1950 and 80 percent of it in 1990; the number of economies with less than 1 percent of GNP (eight in 1950) are now eleven. Moreover, the gap between the more developed and the more backward economies—measured by world exports per capita—also seems to be growing. A comparison with Europe is useful. In the European Union, the gap between the highest and lowest average GNPs was 35 percent in 1960, narrowing to 18 in 1990, while in Latin America analogous figures for the same period show a widening in the gap from 52 to 68. This demonstrates how the policy of trade coordination along the lines laid down by the Latin American Association for Integration's proposals and by various other free trade agreements subscribed to by the region's leading nations tends to reshape relationships between countries. Leading countries will serve as the driving force behind development of the area's less advanced sectors.

What is clear is that a common language, geographical proximity, and a shared need to make exports more competitive (particularly in the area of processed goods) will eventually step up the pace of regional coordination, which, as a prerequisite for the success of current Latin American development, must be consolidated. In fact, without a strong move toward regional coordination, the new general paradigm could result yet again in the defeat of its stated objectives of combining growth, social development, and political democracy.

Note

This chapter was translated by Norman Thomas di Giovanni and Susan Ashe.

8

The United States and Latin America in the World Today

Joseph S. Tulchin

In the euphoria that followed the dramatic razing of the Berlin Wall, in November 1989, President George Bush of the United States triumphantly declared the end of the cold war and summoned the beginning of a "new world order." The phrase was catchy and seemed to match the momentous quality of the events that had preceded the celebration in Berlin. At the time, no one was quite sure what the president's term meant, although it was plain that he intended to convey optimism, a sense that an era of instability and threat was behind us and that all the nations of the globe could look forward to a period of relative peace and goodwill.

Not long after the president had put his rhetorical stamp on the end of the cold war, Francis Fukuyama, the deputy director of the State Department policy planning staff and a former analyst of international affairs at the Rand Corporation, explained that the end of the cold war was, in effect, the end of history. A follower of Hegel, Fukuyama saw in the collapse of the Soviet Union the sudden end of a terrible dialectical struggle for the domination of how the world was to be organized. With that triumph, total and unconditional, the United States and the way of life it represented—democratic capitalism—would sweep all before it.[1] Fukuyama's essay was but one statement in a debate that continues to this day about how best to characterize the post–cold war world.

Events have made a mockery of President Bush's phrase. Indeed, as early as the end of 1992, it was common to dismiss the president's bon mot by referring to the new world *disorder*.[2] In 1995, the peace, the goodwill, the sense of an inertial, almost inevitable drive toward

---

Joseph S. Tulchin is director of the Latin American Program of the Woodrow Wilson Center.

a world community that moved constructively forward—which had been implicit in the president's remarks—are hard to find or even imagine. Everywhere is conflict, disaster, and the threat of worse to come.

But, if there was no consensus about the future, there was no disagreement that the cold war had ended. Indeed, in the aftermath of the dismantling of the Berlin Wall, there was nothing more amazing than the implosion of the Soviet Union. Almost overnight, one of the world's superpowers was reduced to a congerie of independent states, many of which were warring with one another over ethnic identity, territory, economic issues, or a combination of all of these. Even Russia, the largest and most powerful of these states, appeared on the verge of economic collapse and political chaos. Whatever was to follow the cold war would almost certainly not be characterized by a bipolar struggle for hegemony between rival empires that represented conflicting ideological systems.

The precise implications of this change would have to be worked out gradually, on a case by case basis in which each crisis would be used by the parties to evaluate their stake, their commitments, their willingness to act, and their ability to influence the other parties involved to act in a particular manner. Speaking to the Trilateral Commission in 1992, Henry Kissinger remarked on the speed of the current world transformations, saying that, "If we look at history, there have been many periods when there have been changes in the nature of the components that constituted the international order and in the way they interacted with each other. . . . What has not occurred before is the rapidity of change, the global scope of the change, the ability of various regions to communicate instantly with all other regions of the world, and the interconnection—economically and therefore politically—of all the regions."[3]

How would these dramatic changes influence the relations between the United States and Latin America? How would the various nations of Latin America—experiencing a wide variety of economic conditions, but, for the first time in the history of the region, all (except for Cuba) governed by civilian, democratic regimes—react to the changes that had impressed Henry Kissinger?

The debate in the United States over the new world order said very little about Latin America. It was assumed by most authors who studied the international system that the United States would maintain its paramountcy within the Western Hemisphere. Several conservative writers worried that the end of the cold war meant the United States would pay even less attention to Latin America than it had in the recent past, although some noted casually that such disinterest was only right and natural, since Latin America was not likely to present a threat to US interests.[4] Liberals tended to see an opportunity to achieve the partnership between the United States and Latin America that had been frustrated by the myopic policies of the cold war. They argued (or hoped) that the United States would pay more attention to Latin America.[5] During this discussion, the Bush administration concentrated a great deal of energy on the North American Free Trade Treaty, first agreed with Canada and then with Mexico. In fact, the United States and several of the nations in the region seemed to be making economic activities central to their new international relationship. The only policy dealing with Latin America that the Bush administration announced with great fanfare was the Enterprise for the Americas Initiative, which seemed to signal the primacy of economic relations, especially free trade throughout the hemisphere.[6] Some authors, however, took this as an oversold safety precaution against the possibility that Europe and Japan might succeed in consolidating economic blocs that would exclude the United States or at least make it more difficult for the United States to gain access to the markets represented by those blocs.[7]

One policy option appears to have been shunted aside: neoisolationism. The United States was not ready to withdraw from the international arena. The vast military and economic power accumulated since the World War II, together with nearly fifty years' experience in throwing around the nation's geopolitical weight made it hard for the nation to bury its head in the sand. Weakness or geopolitical timidity on the part of other powers, especially Germany and Japan, the United States' major economic rivals, only served to make the last more disposed to strut on the international stage. Moreover, there was the idealistic strain in US policy: a desire to do the right thing and perform humanitarian deeds in the name of democracy. Yugoslavia, the former Soviet Union, Somalia, South Africa, China, the Middle East, Haiti—all were crisis areas that, either because of the human misery they produced or because they threatened to spill over their borders, cried out for external mediation.[8]

After two years of the Clinton administration, a pattern was emerging in the international affairs of the United States that would affect its relations with Latin America. First, there was an emphatic Eurocentrism in the nation's foreign policy concerns. Second, Congress and the public seemed to pay attention to Latin America as a region only in terms of trade or economic relations—what one observer called the NAFTA-ization of inter-American relations.[9] There appeared to be exceptions to this—the attention accorded the crises in dealing with the military dictatorship in Haiti, for example, or the pressure brought to bear by the Cuban-American Foundation to tighten sanctions on Fidel Castro—but these were more issues of domestic politics than debates over foreign policy. Third, there was a reemergence in US policy of a Wilsonian urge to drive the nation to do good works on behalf of democratic capitalism and to teach other nations how to behave and how to enjoy the benefits of the American way of life. Fourth, working against the Wilsonian urge was the Vietnam syndrome, which continued to exert a powerful influence on US thinking in order to ensure that—no matter how worthwhile— the nation did not get bogged down in international adventures. This tendency was reinforced by the Republican capture of both houses of Congress in the elections of 1994. The Republican "Contract with America" is a domestic document with powerful isolationist implications.

The sum of these tendencies suggests that US policy toward Latin America sought to avoid getting involved except where the former's domestic politics made avoidance impossible. Since Latin America could be understood within the global framework of US economic relations, it was a policy that focused on trade and economic issues. Aside from these, the US government seemed to act with extreme caution in handling other items on the inter-American agenda, such as the protection of democracy, the elimination of poverty, the curtailment of drug traffic, environmental protection, the treatment of refugees and illegal immigration, the proliferation of weapons of mass destruction, and corruption. Because the United States did not want to get involved and because neither the government nor the public focused its attention on Latin America, there appeared to be an incipient tendency on the part of the United States to go it alone, acting unilaterally in hemispheric affairs, dealing with the nations of the hemisphere in a bilateral fashion, despite the fact that the Clinton administration began with all sorts of encouragement for multilateral peacekeeping. US action in Mexico's financial crisis of early 1995 is a prime recent example.

Historically, the United States has considered Latin America as something of a nuisance or potential source of trouble. When, at the end of the nineteenth century, export markets became increasingly important to the United States, Latin America was taken more seriously, but the northerners remained concerned about Latin America's instability, which was seen as an excuse for intervention from outside the region as well as a threat to US economic interests. Today, foreign intervention is no longer considered a threat, but instability is still looked on by the United States as a problem. Underdevelopment, too, is worrisome, because it makes Latin America less valuable as a trading partner or recipient of US investment. At the same time, underdevelopment disturbs people in the United States, not only because it is seen as a cause of instability but also as a perpetuator of the human misery that is a constant reproach to the international capitalist system.

How Is Latin America Now to Understand Its Role?

How are the nations of Latin America to deal with current changes in the international system? How are they to define their roles in world affairs? And, inevitably, how will they deal with the United States? First, like the United States, they must come to terms with the transformations described at the opening of this chapter, especially the liberalization of world trade and the increasing globalization of capital, information, and technology. In the same way that Latin American countries differ markedly in size, economic capacity, natural resource endowment, and so forth, so will global changes affect these countries in different ways and degrees. Nevertheless, for all of them, their ability to deal with the changes will determine how they take advantage of the space available to them for autonomous action in the international system.

Crucial to the way in which the nations of Latin America deal with the transition to the post–cold war world will be their ability to estimate the power of the United States. A significant feature of the debate over the relative strength of the United States centered on the rise of Japan and its satellites among the East Asian "tigers" and a unified Europe in the global economy. Some experts were convinced that the world soon would be divided quite sharply into three economic blocs: the Western Hemisphere, led by the United States; Asia, led by Japan; and Europe, led by an institutionalized European Union. This argument was based as much on such factors as efficiency, competitiveness, and growth—where the United States was considered to be lagging badly—as on actual size or a broader definition of power.[10]

Others argued that, while the United States remained—and would remain—the largest economy in the world, its relative weight in the international system would decline as Japan and the European Union grew at a faster rate, and as the world evolved toward interdependence. This prospect suggests a tendency toward multilateral peaceful settlement of disputes. Such a trend, it was argued, will favor Europe economically, enhance collective security organizations, and accelerate the decline of the United States as a dominant power, since economic power or capacity will gradually replace geopolitical power in determining international influence.[11] Finally, there was the realpolitik position. This held firm to the view that because the United States was the only nation with the capacity and the will to project its influence beyond its borders—by military force, if and when necessary—it was the only world power. The Gulf War seemed to lend credence to this position.[12] Most commentators at the end of the 1980s and into 1990 focused on the Big Bang, the date in 1992 when Europe would become a single, unified market. That was to be the date when, symbolically, the United States would no longer be able to extend its influence around the globe. In such a world, the argument ran, Latin America should rethink its dependence on the United States and scramble to line up friends, allies, and patrons in the new trading blocs, especially in Europe.

But shortly after those optimistic essays were written, the Big Bang, while not quite a whimper, was reduced radically. To enumerate some of the factors involved, first the cost to Germany of absorbing the former German Democratic Republic was both to take far more resources and to absorb far more political energy than had been anticipated. At the same time, unemployment in eastern Germany and other factors led to a resurgence of crude neo-Nazi movements, which alarmed all political groups in Germany as well as most of the people of Europe. The Germans, by 1992, were much more preoccupied with domestic issues than they were before 1990 and they were much less confident about their role in world affairs.[13] The civil war in former Yugoslavia became increasingly brutal. The carnage in Bosnia—driven by Serbian desires for ethnic cleansing—seemed to undermine the very behavior and sense of civilized community that lay at the core of the new Europe and that proponents of the European Union assumed would lead to their ascendancy over the United States. Europe, however, seemingly impotent in the face of events in former Yugoslavia, also appeared to be reduced to a catatonic passivity in the face of ethnic conflict and growing economic malaise in the former Soviet Union, of which the conflict in Chechnya is only the most violent evidence; the well publicized starvation in Somalia; or even the gathering criticism of the Maastricht Treaty (on European unification).

At the end of 1992, the world community could act in Somalia only on the coattails of the United States, which agreed to send troops to protect the humanitarian groups delivering food to a starving population preyed upon by rival armed clans. In announcing his decision to send troops to East Africa, President Bush said he was doing so because the United States simply could not stand by and not act. The event held enormous potential significance, and where that put the new "red line" limiting the use of US power was not clear.[14] And in early 1995, the UN exit from Somalia required US military protection and appeared to signal the resumption of clan warfare.

Latin America, meanwhile, had to deal with the harsh fact that, as a region, its share of trade in the world economy had declined from 12 percent in 1960 to 6 percent in 1980 and 3 percent in 1990. During the same period, the region suffered a similar decline as a factor in the US economy, dropping from 25 percent to 13 percent in 1985. Latin America's share in total US overseas investment declined in the same period from 40 percent to 13 percent. In addition, while the debt crisis may have passed, the nations of the region were still digging out from under the burden of a debt that exceeded $500 billion. Repaying that debt, for some of the smaller economies, threatened to stall or stunt economic recovery in the 1990s and complicated the process of economic reform for even the largest of the nations in the region.

The globalization of the world economy, especially finance, was something with which the leaders of Latin America would have to deal. While suggesting greater flexibility and autonomy for Latin America, it also implied the triumph of a capitalist model that many Latin American economists long had believed discriminated against Latin America. It implied, too, that the nations of Latin America would have to throw themselves into an increasingly competitive international economy, and that their historic comparative advantage in the export of primary products was no longer of much value. In this "new" global economy, it appeared that the nations of the region would have to find niches for themselves—whether in primary products, manufacturing, or services—in which they could compete with producers in the industrialized societies of Europe and North America, as well as with the aggressive exporters of East Asia.

A peculiar effect of globalization that complicated Latin American relations with the United States was the increasing and widespread importance of technology. The United States insisted on making access to technology and the protection of intellectual property rights one of the central issues of international trade negotiations. Traditionally, Latin America never had given much attention to these matters. Along with some of the countries in the Pacific basin, the region was notorious for its failure to crack down on violations of copyright. Further, Latin America had never been highly successful in the creation of technology. The key to growth in the 1990s and beyond appeared to be the ability to attract technology, to attract qualified people, and to attract capital. The technologies that mattered most were transportation and information.[15] These were not areas in which Latin America had ever enjoyed a comparative advantage. If the world economy of the future was to be driven by ever more rapid rounds of technological innovation, the countries of the region would have to modernize their economies as quickly as possible.

Another major trend in the international system to which the nations of the region were forced to adapt was the growing significance in the international agenda of what had come to be called global issues. As Henry Kissinger put it in his remarks to the Trilateral Commission in 1992, there are "issues now in the world that go beyond anything previous leaders have had to deal with—environment, population, nuclear issues, problems that genuinely concern all of humanity and that can only be solved on a global basis."[16] Latin Americans did not create these problems, but the issues cannot be avoided.

Some of the emerging global issues represent real threats to the national security of nations in Latin America and create tension in their international relations. The traffic in drugs, for example, has undermined the national sovereignty of Colombia and embarrasses both Peru and Bolivia on account of their lack of capacity to control their national territories. More complicated is the larger question of how to limit international traffic in drugs. The effort to use military force to limit or end production, or to reduce the traffic, complicated bilateral relations between the United States and a number of countries in the region and created considerable tension between nations of the Amazon basin. The kidnapping of a Mexican national on Mexican soil by the US Drug Enforcement Agency embarrassed Mexico. The Salinas government went to great efforts not to let the issue escalate in domestic politics and the affair made it more difficult for President Salinas to push his free market policies and the NAFTA—a result not anticipated by (and certainly not desired by) the Bush administration.

Other global issues that can create tensions between the United States and Latin America are the defense of human rights, the protection of democracy, the proliferation and export of arms of mass destruction, migration, and population control. Central to the discussion of these issues are questions as to what forums can be used to discuss the issues and what institutional mechanisms should be used to adjudicate disputes. How much sovereignty will each nation be willing to cede in order to allow multilateral agencies to deal with these issues? Are these issues in which the various, often conflicting, traditions of international law can help by creating the bases for consensus? Or will the several national traditions divide the hemispheric community?

The directions of general trends in world affairs are hard to predict and the implications for Latin American policy are often obscure. But one obvious change that the end of the cold war will bring to US–Latin American relations is an end to a tightly focused definition of national security in terms of bipolar competition. This inevitably will lead to a redefinition of the terms used in conflict resolution in the hemisphere.[17] How are the nations of Latin America to take advantage of this redefinition in order to maximize their international autonomy?

As a counterpart to the notion that the end of the cold war would create a major role for the United Nations, many in Latin America hoped that the elimination of the Soviet Union as a factor in hemispheric affairs would be an excellent opportunity for the Organization of American States (OAS). Indeed, several of the countries in the hemisphere, led by Argentina and Chile, tried to make the OAS an instrument of protection for democracy and human rights and an effective forum for the discussion of the new global issues, especially the environment.[18] Although significant progress was made in strengthing the OAS, and major steps toward reforming its charter were taken, it was clear that, in the short term, the OAS would not enjoy any more success than the UN as a major new element in the new world order.

Three elements appear to undermine efforts to make the OAS a significant medium for the resolution of hemispheric conflicts. First and foremost of these is the powerful tendency of the US government to act independently, to avoid feeling constrained by other states or multilateral organizations, a tendency only strengthened by the Republican control of Congress after January 1995. Second is the reluctance on the part of many nations in Latin America, especially Mexico, to cede an iota of their national sovereignty to an international organization in which the United States plays a prominent role. Finally, there was some evidence in the 1990s that the sudden end of the rigid, zero-sum, bipolar framework for national security debates would stimulate neonationalist postures in Latin America, just as it had in Europe and in the former Soviet Union.[19]

The challenge for Latin America in the 1990s was to devise new modes of conflict resolution that will not simply recapitulate earlier chapters in inter-American history with the hegemony of the United States, while dealing with the dramatic rise in salience of the new global issues that are shaping the new security agenda. Of particular concern to them will be the following questions: Will the world economy move toward freer trade or will it slip into rigid, exclusionary trading blocs? Will this new economy become a complex, shifting hybrid, requiring extreme flexibility and the heightened capacity to adapt? How will the new world order be governed? As far as the nations of Latin America are concerned, the key to both questions lies in how the United States defines its role in the world.

The Role of the United States

In moving to define its role in world affairs, the United States seemed torn or pulled in two different directions. By the time Bill Clinton took office as president, in 1993, the view that the new world order would be an era of peace governed through the United Nations was held by very few, and their predictions receded farther and farther into the future. The opinion that the United States was the only nation capable of projecting its power beyond its borders seemed to hold sway in discussions about the appropriate posture for the United States in the still uncertain emerging international order, but the notion was countered or questioned internally by a powerful reluctance to pay for international adventures and by a growing insistence that the nation's energies should be devoted to solving problems at home. Clinton's electoral campaign had revolved around this point and, while avoiding direct criticism of anything George Bush had done in foreign policy, insisted it was time to focus on domestic questions.

As far as Latin America is concerned, the end of the cold war certainly marked the end of the tight focus, or definition, of national security in terms of the former bipolar competition with the Soviet Union. Such an obsessively tight focus had distorted US policy in the hemisphere, reaching the point during the first Reagan administration when debates over all facets of policy toward Latin America (military aid, development assistance, defense of democracy and human rights, trade) were decided by the perception of exogenous factors—that is, the cold war—rather than endogenous factors—such as social malaise, state terrorism, and the like.[20] Such a change in the focus of US policy almost immediately led to a shift in how the United States approached conflict resolution in the region.

Nations that had been the subject of intense scrutiny by the United States, welcomed or not—Nicaragua is one example—suddenly found themselves off the front pages of US newspapers and out of the minds of US policymakers. Nicaragua became so insignificant to the Bush administration that Senator Jesse Helms, with little more than a whimper out of the administration, was able to hold up aid to the government of Violeta Chamorro for more than a year and scuttle the appointment of a professional diplomat as ambassador to Managua. Elsewhere in the region, as nations explored the possibilities of multilateral organizations and joint or collaborative ventures (e.g., Mercosur, the Group of Three, the Rio Group, the negotiations between Chile and Argentina, the ongoing series of talks among the presidents of the Central American nations, and the efforts to breathe more life into the Caribbean associations) the US government made approving noises without ever quite expressing enthusiasm for these efforts.[21] Some of this effort was a response to Bush's Enterprise for the Americas Initiative, but a good deal of it was in the nature of probing the limits of the autonomy of action that might be available to the nations of the region once the cold war framework had been removed. Neither the Bush nor the Clinton adminstrations took Latin America seriously enough to go through the exercise of a policy review for the region, but decisionmakers in Washington were unwilling to champion any collective or multilateral initiative by Latin American nations that smacked of limiting US freedom of action—a traditional posture.[22]

One of the greatest beneficiaries of the new sense of freedom to explore new modes of action and their possibilities was the Organization of American States. The United States did not want to arbitrate all interstate disputes in the hemisphere, nor to have its hand forced in any conflict, so for a while, at the beginning of the Bush administration, it looked as if the OAS would become a chosen instrument. Luigi Einaudi, a strong personality and a respected Latin Americanist, was appointed US ambassador to the OAS. In conjunction with a group of Young Turks from Latin America led by Heraldo Muñoz of Chile and Juan Pablo Lohlé of Argentina, Einaudi provided energetic leadership for the OAS. He was a powerful proponent within the State Department to use the OAS as the principal vehicle of US policy in the region.[23]

The alliance among the strongest proponents of democracy in the hemisphere was attractive and congenial to US policy, and the seeming willingness on the part of the OAS to take on tough cases (e.g., the transition to peace in El Salvador, the military coup in Haiti, and a definition of a hemispheric agenda for the environment) meant that the United States could assume a low profile in the area until and unless it had reason to do otherwise. Unfortunately, this quickly proved an illusion.

The first test for the "new" OAS, that of dealing with the military coup in Haiti, proved too complex and involved too many commitments from too many partners in the organization. Several prominent members remained unalterably opposed to an interventionist posture or role for the organization, which had the effect of blunting the force of any collective statement about the crisis. Haiti's president, Jean Bertrand Aristide, was perceived as an uncooperative, uncompromising ally, and no nation in the region would step forward to provide the resources—financial or military—to carry out a solution determined by the majority. Worse, from the US point of view, the OAS was unable to help on the Haitian refugee issue, which soon became a bitter dispute in US domestic politics. The more sensitive the problem became in US politics, the less patience the US government had with the OAS. When the OAS could not agree on a policy, the United States found itself in the unacceptable position of having to go it alone with regard to the growing numbers of Haitians who risked their lives in tiny boats to cross the water to Florida. When the United States tried to get its allies in the OAS to defuse the refugee question by agreeing to take quotas of the Haitians (so that the United States would not have to take them all—a measure that would prove unacceptable to the Congress) there was a babble of explanations as to why this country or that country would not be able to take two thousand or ten thousand refugees. At that point—which coincided with the beginning of the Clinton adminstration—the US government left negotiations with the Haitians to the UN and the OAS, devoting itself to dealing with the domestic fallout of the refugee problem. The crisis was ultimately settled by unilateral US action; first through mediation by Jimmy Carter, and subsequently by occupation of Haiti by US troops in October 1994.

Other items on the agenda of hemispheric conflict resolution—democracy, governance, emigration, civil-military relations, the environment, drug traffic, and poverty—were even more complex, prompting still lower levels of consensus among the membership. Here, the United States was content to allow the OAS to discuss and discuss and discuss, since it was unlikely that anything would result that might embarrass the United States.

The failure of both the Bush and Clinton administrations to adopt with enthusiasm a leadership role for the United States in the OAS was due in part to a long-standing reluctance to allow the organization to compromise US independence of action, and in part to a widespread disdain within the policy-making bureaucracy for the institutional capacity of the OAS. At the same time, the failure was also the result of a genuine confusion within the government as to the direction of foreign policy. In the first place, there was confusion on strategic issues, and uncertainty over what constitutes a threat.

The Department of Defense convened a working group at the end of 1991 to discuss the military's mission in the Western Hemisphere. Through a series of sessions that included commissioned papers from a wide spectrum of civilian analysts, the military and the intelligence community sought some guidance as to what they should be doing in the years ahead.[24] The military, leery of becoming the policemen of the hemisphere, did not want to be drawn casually into seemingly minor confrontations that ought to be dealt with by police forces in the affected countries, especially if there were any hint of domestic disagreement over the use of US forces. Such a prospect was the setting for a quagmire, an unwinnable war, a no-win situation. The public and the Congress shared the reluctance to get sucked into foreign adventures. The so-called Vietnam Syndrome was still powerful in US public opinion and throughout the political spectrum.[25]

The military in the United States took the side of Latin American governments in opposing the use of US troops in efforts to restrict the production and shipment of illicit drugs to the United States from the Southern Hemisphere. Discussions of drug trafficking rarely got far. The United States took the position that the problem was on the supply side; the Latin Americans maintained—with varying degrees of insistence—that the problem was at least half on the demand side. The southerners further argued that solutions focused exclusively on elimination of supply or interdiction of trade were doomed to failure. At one point, the Bush administration offered to send aircraft carriers to the coast of Colombia to prevent planes from leaving Colombian soil en route to clandestine airstrips in the United States; the public outcry in Colombia ended the adventure even before it began.

More complex was the effort to get the Peruvian president, Alberto Fujimori (whose campaign platform had included strong attacks on the drug trade) to accept some form of military support in his efforts to eradicate or reduce the manufacture of cocaine paste on Peruvian soil and its shipment to sites in Colombia or directly to the United States. The Peruvians were anxious to keep the US military involvement quiet and as small as possible. That proved to be ineffective, as the drug lords had private armies that outmanned the joint forces of the Peruvian government and the US Drug Enforcement Agency (DEA). The US military resisted becoming directly involved, although the air force did provide surveillance aircraft for patrols over the area. Even that was ended when the Peruvian air force fired on one of the patrol planes in what was described as a breakdown in communications.[26]

Not surprisingly, nationalists of the left and right opposed giving the US military an important role in fighting the drug lords. Conservatives in the US Congress were frustrated by what they considered to be reluctance on the part of Latin American governments to cooperate with the United States in combating the traffic in drugs.[27] It is significant that the United States avoided unilateral intervention in the border conflict between Peru and Ecuador that burst into hostilities in January 1994. The United States carefully operated together with the so-called "Guarantor Countries"—Argentina, Brazil, and Chile.

The fact of the matter is that the United States did not consider the role of policeman of the hemisphere a worthwhile activity. Whatever the theoretical implications of US hegemony, the government did not want to become responsible for settling conflicts in the region. Latin America seemed to have lost whatever geopolitical or strategic significance it had had during the cold war or before. The initial historical premise for US policing of the Western Hemisphere was to avoid intervention by outside powers whose presence might endanger the United States. Who, from outside, was going to intervene in Latin America in the 1990s? Yugoslavia, the former Soviet Union, the Middle East—those were the areas in which conflicts, if allowed to get out of hand, would threaten the stability of the world and endanger US national interests. No one in official Washington during the Bush and Clinton administrations has believed that political instability in Brazil, an economic meltdown in Argentina, or a "white coup" in Peru could threaten US interests. In the cases of Peru and Venezuela, the United States protested their support for democracy, but the measures taken to back up those declarations were meek and mild compared to what the United States indicated it might do in trouble spots in the Eastern Hemisphere. The US public was more concerned with the crises in Europe and the Middle East than those in Latin America. The only exceptions were Haiti and Cuba, because each of these cases represented the leverage of local Florida groups over national politics, and because the plight of the Haitian refugees stirred the human rights community and portions of the black community.

Haiti, drug traffic, the debt crisis—each of these issues was handled by the government in such a way as to keep them circumscribed, to reduce US commitments of resources, and to make sure that they did not impinge on broader areas of the nation's concern. Protestations of Latin America's importance to the United States were based on projections of future economic interest. Some argued that a revived Latin America would be a major market for the United

States and a perfect field for US investments, especially if the European Union proved to be less open than the GATT negotiations promised, but until the revival took place, the fact remained that Europe and Asia were both far more important to the US economy. Other arguments in support of Latin America's significance to the United States, such as a shared historical experience, shared democratic aspirations, cultural affinities, and feelings of brotherhood, always seemed to lose out in the setting of priorities to more pragmatic, immediate considerations, in which strategic concerns seemed more clearly defined.

Further complicating US policy in the hemisphere during the Bush and Clinton administrations has been a curious resurgence of Wilsonianism, that urge (born of a certitude that the US system is the best—and the best for everyone everywhere) to teach the benefits of liberal democracy to anyone, even by force. Emerging from the final years of the cold war and from the bitter internal debate over intervention in El Salvador and Nicaragua, new domestic and international alliances had formed that were ferociously activist on matters of human rights and the defense of democracy. The National Endowment for Democracy (NED) interpreted its successful intervention in Chile, in favor of democracy in the plebiscite organized by the military dictator Augusto Pinochet, as proof that it was possible to intervene on the side of democracy without stirring a nationalist backlash (except on the part of the bad guys, which did not count, or not for very much)—and all without upsetting the bipartisan coalition in Congress that provided its funding. The NED, looking around for other fields to conquer, increased pressure on Cuba even as it mounted technical assistance missions to nations in the former Soviet bloc in order to teach the countries how to organize judiciaries, write legal codes, and establish political parties and the other institutions of democracy. The Democracy Project in the U.S. Agency for International Development (AID) quickly became the largest single foreign aid program of the US government and the core of AID's policy of "sustainable democracy."[28]

The defense of democracy was a policy around which Democrats and Republicans could build coalitions. The virtues of democracy brought liberals and conservatives together. Both sides seemed to be convinced of the universality of democratic values as well as of the efficacy of collective action in preserving, protecting, or even creating the institutional mechanisms of democracy. Some who had been staunchly opposed to intervention in the 1980s began to assume the postures of Wilsonian interventionism.[29] The Cuban American community used the democracy issue to insinuate itself into the mainstream debate on foreign policy and to win allies among human rights groups and others who for years had shunned the Miami Cubans as selfish reactionaries. It was no accident that Bill Clinton, as presidential candidate, indicated his support for the Toricelli bill, which banned trade with Cuba by foreign subsidiaries until Fidel Castro made clear steps to restore democracy and that insiders spoke of the Cuban-American "litmus test" for the new adminstration's appointees who would have anything to do with Latin America. For nearly a month after the Clinton inauguration, the Cuban-American lobby seemed to control the formulation of Latin American policy.[30] Cuba was excluded from the December 1994 summit in Miami and increasingly isolated within the hemisphere because of US pressure. The conservation supporters of democracy and the more progressive advocates of US intervention against dictators had trouble agreeing over how the United States should play its role as protector of democracy in the hemisphere.

In the aftermath of the cold war, and with the transition to democracy well advanced in the region, the human rights community consciously set out to reinvent itself and to define its new mission now that the United States apparently was not going to engage in clandestine interventions in the hemisphere or in operations supportive of dictatorships or other regimes that blatantly violated the human rights of their citizens. Organizations such as the Washington Office on Latin America (WOLA), Americas Watch, and various church-related human rights groups sought ways to remain effective in helping the forces of democracy in the hemisphere consolidate their strength and extend more widely into the populations of Latin American countries. Transnational nongovernmental organizations (NGOs) had come to play a critical role in defining Latin American interests as well as in influencing US policy. Theirs, too, was a posture of universalism and activism. It was a position that staked out the moral high ground for the United States and justified intervention for just cause, as in Somalia.

The problem was, however, that the NGOs had served also to confuse the line between domestic and international issues. They were anxious to get the UN involved, but sensitive to the need to define carefully the parameters for multilateral action, and they were conscious of the ambiguity toward the UN within the US foreign policy establishment.[31] While there really was no dissent over the importance of human rights, the question was how to intervene to accomplish special purposes, without getting caught in one of those quagmires. Intervention was not so simple.

Enterprise for the Americas Initiative

If the Bush administration was ambivalent over how to export democracy in the hemisphere, it had no doubts about how to solve Latin America's economic problems. The free trade treaty with Canada seemed to be going well. The US position in the GATT negotiations clearly favored freer trade. Mexico was about to join Canada and the United States in forming NAFTA. Why not extend the benefits of NAFTA to the entire hemisphere? This seemed to fit in with the efforts of the multilateral lending agencies to push the governments of Latin America to get their economic houses in order, to restructure their economies and modernize their policies, and to make their nations more competitive. It was in this context that, on 27 June 1990, President Bush announced the Enterprise for the Americas Initiative (EAI).

The administration emphasized that the president's new policy was part of a worldwide phenomenon—part of the broad swing toward market economies and democratic policies. According to Roger B. Porter, one of Bush's advisers on economic matters, the undertaking was part of a "vision for Latin America that is built on a foundation of partnership: partnership between Latin America and the Caribbean on the one hand and the United States on the other; partnership among the governments in the Hemisphere and their private sector; and partnership among the private sectors of the countries in the region."[32] This official explanation of the EAI recognized that there were scant government resources involved. That was the point: the EAI was about markets, eliminating barriers to trade and to entrepreneurship, and reducing statism. "The challenge to Latin governments under the Bush initiative," Porter said in a speech to the Americas Society in the fall of 1990, "is to remove obstacles to efficiently functioning markets and to create a climate for entrepreneurship." States should not be involved in production, but should "implement regulations which safeguard foreign investments and facilitate the entry and exit of capital."[33]

President Bush, by nature an optimist, saw a global trend toward market economics and democratic politics. He was particularly encouraged by the movement toward freer international trade, believing profoundly, as he did, in the efficacy of untrammeled international exchange. This was reflected in the government's recognition of the consensus with respect to the transformation of the international market. Taking up a view long advocated by the international lending agencies and the International Monetary Fund, and now legitimized by a broad consensus among academic economists, the so-called Washington Consensus stressed the virtues of the free market and the need to restructure the command economies of the former Socialist bloc and the protectionist economies of the Third World along lines congenial to the policies of the industrialized nations of the developed West.[34]

According to this view, the end of the cold war ushered in a trend toward openness in the international economy. This openness was based on increasingly free trade and growing ease of movement of capital, labor, and information across national boundaries. Such restructuring, or reform, by the developing nations would permit their reinsertion into the increasingly competitive world economy, where efficiency and comparative advantage appeared to be the keys to success.

The cold war over, the nations of Eastern Europe were free to join in a movement already well advanced in the Western Hemisphere, where, with the exception of Cuba, each nation was ruled by civilian, elected governments, an alignment unique in the region's history. Moreover, many of the governments had set out on economic reforms of profound significance, turning away from import substitution models of development that had dominated policymaking virtually since the Great Depression and that had been an article of faith since the 1950s: the trend was toward opening their economies to the international market. The Washington Consensus seemed global in its reach. It was the economists' version of Fukuyama's End of History.

Despite these trends, President Bush had been upset by the lament of the presidents of the Andean nations with whom he had met early in 1990 to discuss the vexing issue of drug traffic. Bush had gone to the meeting in Cartagena expecting enthusiastic cooperation from his Latin American colleagues. Instead, the leaders of Bolivia, Peru, and Colombia had reported to him that their countries—and the other countries of the region—were caught in an economic tailspin. They reported that the 1980s had been a lost decade for Latin America. The region had gone backward in economic terms, pinned down by the heavy burden of the enormous unpaid international debt, which had brought the flow of private capital to a standstill and dragged most of the hemisphere into a recession that was undermining the new and fragile democracies. In the face of severe recession, the civilian governments were unable to raise the revenue to satisfy the legitimate needs of their populations.

To compound the problem, the restructuring programs that were imposed on Latin America by the international banks as a condition for renewed loans (and sometimes by the US Treasury as a condition for credits by the Export-Import Bank or other federal agencies) were sapping the strength of the state. This came precisely at a time when, to consolidate the fledgling moves toward democracy and respond to legitimate social needs such as staggering unemployment and to threats such as drug traffic, environmental degradation, or terrorism (all items at the top of the US agenda for the hemisphere) a strong state was needed.

President Bush was not attracted to the idea of proposing a program of official aid. Such a program would go against his own philosophy, and he knew that even if he were to adopt one he would have a tough time selling it to Congress and to the US people, who— in the toils of a lingering recession and the costs of the savings-and-loan scandal—were leery of increased foreign aid. Historically, with the exception of the Alliance for Progress, the United States had responded to Latin American requests for economic help by urging them to open their markets and allow US capital to solve their problems. "Trade not aid," was the response of US officials after the World War II to Latin American colleagues who asked for a hemispheric equivalent of the Marshall Plan. Bush was not the first US president to believe in the magical healing powers of the international market.

These general concerns were focused for the president and his immediate advisers on the specific case of Mexico, whose young, Harvard-educated president, Carlos Salinas de Gortari, had embarked on a bold reform program designed to open the Mexican economy, jump-starting it with massive infusions of foreign capital and privatizations. For many years, to the United States Mexico had been a special case. Aside from the obvious ties created by intertwined histories, a two-thousand-mile border, and a high level of economic interdependence, the two countries were forced to confront together the most significant movement of migrants—legal and illegal—in the hemisphere. As Texans, President Bush and secretary of state James Baker had a greater awareness of Mexico than had most people in the United States. They also had an acute sense that they should do something about and for Mexico. And again as Texans, they tended to confuse the rest of Latin America with Mexico. What was good for Mexico undoubtedly would be good for the rest of the region.

Meeting at the president's ranch in southern Texas, Bush and Baker took into account their recent decision to begin talks with Mexico for a free trade zone, which, when added to Canada, would constitute the future North American Free Trade Area. They also thought about the president's forthcoming trip to South America, scheduled for September.[35] What emerged seemed to be the perfect package. The result of policy planning within the Treasury Department by a small group called together by Secretary Nicholas Brady, the ensuing plan (aimed at Mexico but to include the rest of the hemisphere) was designed to deal with the major preoccupations of Latin America—debt, trade, and economic well-being.

In and of itself, the Enterprise for the Americas Initiative accomplished little. A more serious problem was that it was oversold in Latin America.[36] Even if all barriers to trade with the United States were to have been eliminated, nontariff barriers included, Latin American exports to the United States would increase by only 8 percent. That amount would not have been enough either to solve Latin America's economic woes or fuel the engines of growth for very long.

The indirect gains, however, were—and are—significant. At the very least, in a worst-case scenario, the possibility of a free trade area in the hemisphere would protect the Latin American nations against a resurgence of US protectionism, although nontariff barriers have become so complex and the asymmetry between the US economy and the economies of the Latin American nations so vast that true free trade would, under the best of circumstances, be decades away and, under more difficult circumstances, be hopelessly delayed.

Still, the EAI has provided important indirect benefits, even if we take a harsh or cynical view of its accomplishments in the short term. There has been a palpable increase in investor confidence in Latin America, as shown by the impressive demand for securities on a growing number of exchanges in the region, and there has been significant flow of private capital into a few of the countries, mainly Chile and Mexico, although in the wake of the Mexican currency crisis, this flow has slowed considerably. If the EAI has provided a buttress for free trade policies that are historically anomolous, politically vulnerable, and subject to domestic attack, then, by making the economies of the Latin American nations more competitive in the international marketplace, the plan may prove to be a self-fulfilling prophesy of the most positive sort.

Perhaps most important, in rushing to expand the hemisphere free trade area, the EAI gave the nations of Latin America a powerful stimulus to intraregional integration efforts, pushing them further toward realization than at any previous time. As projects such as Mercosur and the Andean Pact are brought to fruition, they will strengthen the economies of Latin America at a critical time and prove to be a powerful support for the self-esteem of the peoples of the hemisphere.

Ironically, by pushing the Latin American nations to restructure their economies, then leading them to expect great things from an EAI that was given a splashy inauguration, then suggesting that a NAFTA for the hemisphere was the solution to their problems, and finally frustrating them by bureaucratic inadequacy and partisan wrangling, the United States may end up strengthening Latin American regionalism.[37] Historically, the United States has preferred to deal with Latin American nations on an individual basis and has gone to great lengths to discourage joint or multilateral efforts. Today, in the aftermath of the cold war, the United States needs Latin America to join it in the settlement of hemispheric disputes, just as it needs European or other allies to deal effectively with crises in Yugoslavia, Cambodia, Iraq, or elsewhere, whether through the United Nations or other forms of collective effort. In the Western Hemisphere, the United States needs allies to deal with crises in Haiti and Peru, allies to deal effectively with drug traffic, with terrorism, or with threats to the environment. That need for allies, for partners, may produce some changes in US policy that were not entirely anticipated and that run counter to the United States' historic need for a free hand in hemispheric action. The Bush administration gave every indication that it preferred to act alone. Historically, the Democrats have been more inclined toward multilateral cooperation with Latin America.

The end of the cold war brought a remarkable reemergence in the United States of some traditional approaches to dealing with Latin America. These seemed to be drawn from the distant past and to rely upon deeply felt and widely shared assumptions about US relations with the rest of the hemisphere. Briefly, such attitudes—they cannot be called a coherent or conscious policy so much as a set of concurrent attitudes—include an aversion to interference by outsiders, a compulsion to prevent any instability that threatens the United States, and a desire to preserve US autonomy of action so that its global interests are not compromised. Taken together, such an outlook—if formulated deliberately as policy—would indicate a hemispheric hegemon whose major preoccupations were elsewhere, a hegemon that preferred not to get involved if at all possible, and a hegemon that would like to reserve the region as a kind of preserve, a safety area that might be redefined as an economic bloc if that proved necessary. In dealing with Latin America, such a traditional posture would emphasize what the Founding Fathers called propinquity. The United States would be primarily concerned with the countries or issues closest to its territory and most likely to threaten the nation's well-being. Thus, Mexico gets more attention than Brazil and, therefore, the broad, intense discussion of and support for the NAFTA.

Of course, new technologies and new global issues have altered our sense of distance, but the same rules appear to apply today as have applied over the past two hundred years. Emigration is currently a source of deep concern, and countries that send large numbers of immigrants to our shores are considered close in every sense. The importance of environmental issues in US politics is influenced by the public perception of how close or immediate the threat is. The destruction of the Amazon rainforest seems more immediate than the problem of acid rain in Canada, more threatening than the destruction of the rainforest in Puerto Rico or Costa Rica, and—now that the Soviet Union is not seen as a party to the conflict—much more threatening than civil disorder in Nicaragua. The debate over Cuba seemed to have less to do with foreign policy and international affairs than it did with the extraordinary leverage over the US political discussion exercised by the Cuban-American Foundation, which suggests that countries in Latin America are close to the extent that they become part of the domestic political debate.

The implications of this concept of distance seemed to be that the farther from the United States, the more removed from the nation's attention, the greater the autonomy of action available to the countries of Latin America. Actions by one country may be seen as unobjectionable; the same actions by another country may be considered dangerous. By the same token, similar actions by the same country at two different moments might well elicit different responses from the United States. In calculating foreign policy responses toward Latin America, so much depends on how the situation is perceived in the United States and how deeply enmeshed the issue becomes in US domestic politics. In less than two years, Nicaragua went from an issue central to the foreign policy debate in the United States to a nation pleading for attention from the U.S. government.[38]

Latin American Options

How was Latin America to deal with the new world order after the cold war? What were the options available to the nations of the region? In one sense, they found the end of the cold war liberating, for it would no longer be necessary for them to define their own national security and to have their policies evaluated and defined in terms of US perceptions of their relevance or impact on the bipolar struggle. On the other hand, while it was maddening and, in the last analysis, demeaning to define one's national security in terms of the perception of another nation, the bipolar competition did allow for a certain amount of playing off of one great power against the other.

Such gambits had their cost—the United States never took kindly to Latin American flirtations with the Soviet Union—but they brought some benefits as well, at least in the short term. Trade with the Soviet Union, as Argentina engaged in when no one else would buy its grain, was less objectionable than establishing links that carried political or military implications. Cuba, of course, was the most extreme example.[39] Once the Soviet Union began to pull back from its Cuban commitments, the United States responded with vindictiveness. Instead of welcoming Cuba back in the hemispheric fold, the United States tightened its embargo with the Toricelli Bill and threatened subsidiaries of US corporations that traded with Cuba. The signals to Latin America were mixed and difficult to interpret.[40]

But there was as much, if not more, confusion in Latin America as in the United States over what might be an appropriate foreign policy in the post–cold war world. Several important efforts were made to define national security policy in an autonomous fashion.[41] And, in many countries, a great deal of attention was paid to what was known as the reinsertion into the international system. However, for the most part, the discussion was driven by economic issues. Again, the framework seemed to be determined from outside the region in the so-called Washington Consensus. The main concern was to reinsert Latin America in the international market. As had been the case through most of the cold war, the nations of Latin America were anxious about their development model. A Chilean general commented that "underdevelopment was the principal security threat to Latin America."[42] In such a case, Latin Americans did not seem to have much choice. How were they to be competitive in the global market? Modernization was the key, and the modalities of modernization were taken for granted. The Latin American dilemma seemed all the more acute as the nations of Eastern Europe and the former Soviet Union rushed to create the trappings of democracy and free market capitalism. How frustrating for Latin American leaders to do everything possible to hurry the restructuring of their economies, at cruel social cost, only to see potential investors rush to Eastern Europe and hesitate to venture south. Meanwhile, these leaders waited and waited for their own investors to bring home the billions of dollars stashed abroad that were needed to stimulate and revive the economies of their own countries.[43] Some people in Latin America, worried about the social cost of restructuring or unconvinced of the virtues of the Washington Consensus, began to explore alternative models and to look for other "possible capitalisms."[44]

By the beginning of the 1900s, the requirements for successful reinsertion in the global market and a key to Latin America's future success in the international system appeared to be set by what we might call an international code of good behavior. Rarely explicit, its elements were obvious in the reactions of the United States and other major economic powers to dealings with the developing nations.

First and foremost, it was necessary to have a democratic government. Second, it was essential to guarantee the sanctity of property and to welcome capital in its various forms: the code for this was to have an "open" economy. Every nation in the hemisphere, even Cuba, tried to be more open than it had been, although the pace and comprehensiveness of the opening varied widely from country to country. Finally, and most difficult, it was necessary to be "transparent" in the conduct of international affairs and in the protection of human and property rights. This was a touchy subject, because it ran into a combination of corruption and long-standing local protection measures—for example, for the computer industry in Brazil and the pharmaceutical industry in Argentina. It became clear that traditional forms of influence peddling in Latin America could become a limiting factor in the creation of new markets and, more important, in a nation's capacity to attract new investment.[45]

To maximize their autonomy in the world marketplace, the nations of Latin America had to be competitive. This meant that they had to produce products at attractive prices. It also meant that they had to prepare their labor force to produce new products in an efficient and competitive fashion. Otherwise, they would be condemned to perpetual exportation of primary products, prices for which were at best unstable and more often soft, or else held to serve as cheap labor *maquiladoras*. The escape from the cheap labor trap would be through the creation of a labor force capable of handling increasingly sophisticated manufactured products. This, however, raised the thorny questions of technology transfer and education reform. Would the nations of Latin America be able to gain access to the technology necessary to produce the manufactures they might want? Would Latin Americans be able to restructure their education systems to adapt to new global demands?[46]

Even if Latin Americans followed all the prescriptions of the international lending agencies and opened their economies, and even if these nations were transparent in their international dealings and remained steadfast in their political democracy, their capacity to exert influence in the international system—the space they would enjoy within the system—would be determined in part also by their ability to deal with their own increasing poverty. The debt crisis and the restructuring programs together had forced severe restrictions in government welfare programs and, in some cases, caused recession. The restrictions contributed to massive increases in the incidence of poverty and, in some countries, to more marked inequities in the distribution of income.[47]

In some cases, the perception of inequity, together with corruption, was a volatile mix. It produced two attempted coups against the regime of Carlos Andrés Pérez in Venezuela and social disturbances throughout the hemisphere.[48] A democratic government's capacity for action in the international system was seriously restricted by the spread of poverty among its people and by its own inability to deal with that poverty. Moreover, the threat to democracy that growing social inequity represented could so focus the attention of a government on domestic issues that it might become weaker in its international dealings. Its international space would be reduced. Similarly, its ability to speak with authority in an international forum would be influenced by such things as social inequity and corruption and the perceived propriety of its democratic government. Costa Rica is the most extreme example of a country that has based its international role on the consolidation of its democracy. The government of Carlos Menem, in Argentina, tried to use a single-minded defense of democracy as an instrument of foreign policy to increase the influence of Argentina in international organizations such as the OAS.

No matter what their economic strategy, no matter what their view of how the post–cold war world will be organized, the nations of Latin America will have to deal with the fact that the United States will continue to be the unrivaled hegemonic power in the hemisphere. Whatever their view of the debate over the decline of the United States, there is no challenger to the United States in the Western hemisphere. Even in the cases where Europe or Japan have a larger share of a nation's trade than the United States, or where one or another of the rival economic blocs is making signficant investments in the economy of a Latin American nation, neither Japan nor any of the nations of Europe is interested in, or capable of, exercising influence within the hemisphere that comes remotely close to hegemony. The Latin Americans will have to deal with the United States or come up with an independent posture that takes the United States into account. For good or for ill, Japan and Europe are preoccupied with what is happening in South east Asia, Eastern Europe, and the former Soviet Union. They accord even less attention and priority to Latin America than does the United States. Disturbances in the Eurasian landmass, especially in the former Soviet Union, elicit a markedly different reaction than disorder in Brazil or Kenya. This disparity is likely to hold at least for the next decade.

Relative inattention is damaging to the national ego, but it also represents a historically unique opportunity to create a role in international affairs. US preoccupation with Europe means that Latin America can exercise considerable autonomy in the definition of its role in world affairs. So long as they are democratic, and so long as they do not glaringly violate the emerging Wilsonian code of international behavior, the nations of Latin America will have considerable autonomy to help define the nature of the new national security agenda. The United States will be more than happy to cede leadership to a democratic Latin America in an equitable solution to such problems as Haiti, Cuba, drug traffic, and the entire gamut of global issues. The US military has indicated that it is willing to collaborate with Latin American partners in its expanding "nontraditional" mission in the hemisphere.[49] Confusion in the United States over what its role in world affairs should be and a lack of consensus on the value of multilateral organizations to enforce the international code of behavior and to resolve conflicts makes that autonomy greater still.

The dilemma for Latin America is that, never before having been in a position to assume real autonomy or real responsibility, it is seriously inhibited. There is little awareness that in order to exercise responsibility in world affairs—to carve out a role of increasing influence—a nation must be prepared to sacrifice some measure of sovereignty. This is difficult for Latin American countries, which have exerted most of their international effort since independence to protect their sovereignty, particularly, in this century, from the United States, and will not easily give any of it up. The "Declaration of Santiago," in which nations of the region pledge to act against a military coup in any country, appears to be just the right sort of mechanism through which the Latin American nations can take their destiny into their own hands. The question is, How will it be used—if at all?[50] It was applied successfully by an ad hoc multilateral group in Guatemala in 1993 but could not be invoked with effect in dealing with Haiti.

The OAS is both a key to and a reflection of what is happening in Latin America and in the hemisphere as a whole. Indeed, it is fair to say that the OAS today is also a reflection of what is happening globally. Whatever else it might be or become, the OAS is currently a critical forum in which the nations of Latin America define their own security. For nearly one hundred years, these countries have been searching for a way of living together and, simultaneously, a way to curb the tendency of the United States to act unilaterally within the hemisphere, often at the expense of the national interests and even the sovereignty of one or more of the other nations of the Americas. The central question has become: Will the nations of Latin America define their security in strictly national terms or in terms which take advantage of, or require some measure of, regional co-operation or integration?[51] Whatever the answer, it appears fairly certain that in the forseeable future the ability to control or inhibit the individual action of the United States will depend upon the ability of Latin American countries to cooperate with one another in either regional or subregional groups. In the short run, it may prove easier for them to operate in ad hoc groups in which the common interest is clear—for example,the Esquipulas group, the Group of Rio, or the Group of Three—rather than in the OAS itself, which is hampered by its comprehensive membership, its historical baggage, and its institutional clumsiness.

Will Latin Americans succeed in defining their own positions with regard to the emerging global agenda so that they can accommodate or combine their respective positions with that of the United States? Or will they remain reactive—responding to the US definition of how the hemisphere should deal with these issues, and to the definition by the United States of its national interests? Some Latin American analysts suggest that Latin American definitions may prove divisive and not lead to greater cohesiveness.[52] In this context, it is clear that the OAS can do no more than the member states have the will to do and that smaller, more flexible groups may have greater leverage.

These possibilities represent an historic opportunity—and present Latin America with a fearsome challenge. Never before have the nations of Latin America had a similar chance to define their roles in the world community and to contribute in a meaningful, substantial fashion to the shaping of the hemispheric community. They must act—and soon—or the opportunity may pass and a new framework will be imposed on them that could reduce their autonomy to less than it is today or what it was in the past. The United States will not willingly or deliberately remain in the state of confusion in which it finds itself in the mid-1990s. More than at any time since their independence, the nations of Latin America have their destiny in their own hands.

Notes

1. F. Fukuyama, "The End of History?" *The National Interest* 16 (summer 1989). The essay, with the comments, and rejoinder to the comments was converted into a book, *The End of History and The Last Man* (New York: Free Press, 1992).

2. For example, Kim R. Holmes, "The New World Disorder," *The Heritage Lectures;* also the Staff of the Heritage Foundation, *Making the World Safe for America: A U.S. Foreign Policy Blueprint* (Washington DC: Heritage Foundation, 1992). For another view of the same subject, see Stanley Hoffman, "Delusions of World Order," *New York Review of Books,* 9 April 1992.

3. Kissinger, "Unsolved Problems," in *Lisbon 1992* (Trilateral Commission, 1992).

4. Mark Falcoff, article in the *Washington Post;* and Holmes, "New World Disorder."

5. Robert Pastor, *Whirlpool: U.S. Foreign Policy toward Latin America and the Caribbean* (Princeton: Princeton University Press, 1992); Abraham Lowenthal, "Latin America and the New Winds," *Miami Herald,* 25 March 1990; "The United States and Latin America in the 1990s: Changing U.S. Interests and Policies in a New World" (Washington DC: Inter-American Dialogue, May 1991); and "The United States and Latin America in a New World," *North-South,* (June-July 1992). See also Peter Hakim, "The United States and Latin America: Good Neighbors Again?" *Current History* 91, no. 562 (Feb. 1992); and Richard Feinberg, "Latin America: Back on the Screen," *International Economic Insights* (July-Aug. 1992). Looking beyond the Bush administration, Inter-American Dialogue indicated that "opportunities for sustained cooperation [never] had been greater." *Convergence and Community: The Americas in 1993. A Report of the Inter-American Dialogue* (Washington DC: Aspen Institute, 1992).

6. Roger B. Porter, "The Enterprise for the Americas Initiative: A New Approach to Economic Growth," *Journal of Interamerican Studies* 32, no. 4 (winter 1990): 2; Peter Hakim, "The Enterprise for the Americas Initiative," *Washington Quarterly* 15, no. 2 (spring 1992). Also, see Hakim, "The Enterprise for the Americas Initiative, What Washington Wants," *Brookings Review* (fall 1992).

7. Tulchin,"The Enterprise for the Americas Initiative," in Roy Green, ed., *United States Trade Relations* (Boulder: Westview, 1993).

8. One survey of post–cold war approaches to foreign policy giving greater importance to the neonationalist position is Alan Tonelson, "Beyond Left and Right," *The National Interest* (winter 1993–1994). It is my view that the internationalists still dominate the academic debate as well as the policy community.

9. Interview with Moisés Naím, Carnegie Endowment, 18 January 1993.

10. Paul Kennedy, *Imperial Overreach* (New Haven: Yale University Press, 1990); David Calleo, *Declining Hegemon* (Baltimore: JHU Press, 1991); Samuel P. Huntington, "The U.S.—Decline or Renewal?" *Foreign Affairs* 67, no. 2 (1988–1989).

11. Robert O. Keohane and Joseph S. Nye, Jr., *Power and Interdependence,* 2d ed. (New York: Scott, Foresman, 1989), Nye, "Arms Control After the Cold War," *Foreign Affairs* 68, no. 5 (winter 1989–1990) and a few European authors in 1990 anticipated Europe's arrival on the scene as a major force,

although they differed among themselves as to the consequences this might have for the polarity of power in the international system. On the role of the United Nations and collective security, see Thomas G. Weiss and Meryl A. Kessler, eds., *Third World Security in The Post–Cold War Era* (Boulder: Lynne Rienner, 1991); and Weiss, ed., *Collective Security in a Changing World* (Boulder: Lynne Rienner, 1993). For a fairly optimistic view of the United Nations, see the Stanley Foundation, *The United Nations and Multilateral Sanctions: New Options for US Policy?* (Muscatine, IA: Stanley Foundation, 1992).

12. John Lewis Gaddis, "Toward the Post–Cold War World," *Foreign Affairs* 70, no. 2 (1990–1991); and Charles Krautheimer, "The Unipolar Moment," *Foreign Affairs* 70, no. 1 (1991); Robert W. Tucker and David C. Hendrickson, *The Imperial Temptation: The New World Order and America's Purpose* (New York: The Council on Foreign Relations, 1992); and Susan Strange, "The Persistent Myth of Lost Hegemony," *International Organization*, 41, no. 3 (autumn 1987). For an interesting collection of views, with some historical perspective, see Michael J. Hogan, ed., *The End of the Cold War* (New York: Cambridge University Press, 1992).

13. For example, see the talk by W. R. Smyser, "Germany's Domestic Situation and U.S. Relations," Institute for Defense Analyses, 12 Aug. 1992.

14. *New York Times*, 5 Dec. 1992, p. 1.

15. John Kasarda, "Jobs, Migration, and Emerging Urban Mismatches," in Michael G. H. McGeary and L. E. Lynn, Jr., eds., *Urban Change and Poverty* (Washington DC: National Academy Press, 1988); and Kasarda, "Structural Factors Affecting the Location and Timing of Urban Underclass Growth," *Urban Geography* 11, no. 3 (1990).

16. Kissinger, "Unsolved Problems."

17. Augusto Varas, "Global Transformations and Peace: Arms Control, Disarmament and the Resolution of Conflict in the Western Hemisphere in the Post–Cold War Period. A Framework for Analysis," manuscript prepared for a workshop at the Woodrow Wilson Center (WWC), 16 Nov. 1992.

18. José Baena Soares,"The Future of the Organization of American States," Woodrow Wilson Center, 15 April 1991; Heraldo Muñoz, *Environment and Diplomacy in the Americas* (Boulder: Lynne Rienner, 1992); speech by Ambassador Hernán Patiño Mayer at Tufts University, 6 Feb. 1992.

19. A. Varas, "Los nuevos parametros estrategicos en el cono sur," paper presented at the North-South conference, "Mercosur and Strategic Issues in the Southern Cone," Miami, 7 Dec. 1992.

20. Lars Schoultz, *National Security Policy in U.S.—Latin American Relations* (Princeton: Princeton University Press, 1986); Schoultz, *Human Rights and United States Policy toward Latin America* (Princeton: Princeton University Press, 1981); and Luis Maira, ed., *Estados Unidos. Una Visión Latinoamericana* (Mexico: CIDE, 1984); Walter LaFeber, *Inevitable Revolutions* (New York: Norton, 1983); and Thomas Carothers, *In the Name of Democracy* (Berkeley: Univ. of California Press, 1991).

21. Anthony Bryan, "A Wider Caribbean . . . at Last?" *North-South*, 1, no. 5 (February–March 1992); Jorge I. Dominguez, Robert A. Pastor, and R. DeLisle Worrell, *The Caribbean Prepares for the 21st Century* (Boston: World Peace Foundation, 1986); also in Robert A. Pastor and Richard Fletcher, "The Caribbean in the 21st Century," *Foreign Affairs* 70, no. 3 (summer 1991); Andrés Serbin, "The Caribbean: Myths and Realities for the 1990s," *Journal of Interamerican Studies* 32, no. 2 (summer 1990); and Serbin, "The

Caricom States and the Group of Three: A New Partnership Between Latin America and the Non-Hispanic Caribbean?" *Journal of Interamerican Studies* 33, no. 2 (summer 1991); and speech by the Jamaican ambassador to the United States, Richard Bernal, reprinted in *Enterprise for the Americas Initiative*, Report no. 8 (Woodrow Wilson Center, Sept. 1992), and Bernal's statement before the House Committee on Small Business, "Impact of NAFTA on the Economic Development of the Caribbean and U.S./Caribbean Trade," 16 Dec. 1992; Roberto Bouzas, "A US-Mercosur Free Trade Area," in Sylvia Saborio, ed., *The Premise and the Promise: Free Trade in the Americas* (Washington DC: ODC, 1992); and "The Southern Cone Countries in the International Political Economy" (Buenos Aires: FLACSO, 1992); Felix Peña, "Competitividad, Democracia e Integración en las Americas," paper presented at seminar organized by the Fundação G. Vargas, 21 Aug. 1992.

22. Tulchin, "Enterprise for the Americas Initiatives."

23. See the remarks by Luigi Einaudi and Heraldo Muñoz in Baena Soares, "The Future."

24. L. Erik Kjonnerod, ed., *Evolving U.S. Strategy for Latin America and the Caribbean* (Washington DC: National Defense University Press, 1992); and the series of publications by the National Defense University, as, for example, Samuel J. Watson, ed., "Proceedings of the Latin American Strategy Development Workshop Series" (May 1992).

25. Tulchin, "Estados Unidos y la crisis en Centroamerica: una perspectiva histórica," in Juan del Aguila, et al., *Realidades y Posibilidades de la Relaciones entre España y America en los Ochenta* (Madrid: ICI, 1986).

26. *New York Times*, 23 Oct. 1992. For a comprehensive treatment of the drug issues, see the special issue, "Drug Trafficking Research Update," *Journal of Interamerican Studies* 34, no. 3 (fall 1992); and Peter H. Smith, ed., *Drug Policy in the Americas* (Boulder: Westview, 1992); and "United States Drug Policy Toward Latin America," WWC working paper no. 194 (1991). For a Latin American view of the issue, see Diego Cardona y Juan Gabriel Tokatlian, "El sistema mundial en los noventa," *Colombia Internacional*, no. 13 (January–March 1991); Adrian Bonilla, "Teoría de las relaciones internacionales como discurso político: El caso de la guerra de las drogas," *Colombia Internacional*, no. 15 (July–Sept. 1991). More sensational treatments are Clare Hargreaves, *Snowfields: The War on Cocaine in the Andes* (New York: Holmes & Meier, 1992); and Michael Smith, ed., *Why People Grow Drugs: Narcotics and Development in the Third World* (London: Panos, 1992); and Renssalaer W. Lee III, *The White Labyrinth: Cocaine and Political Power* (Putgers: Transaction Press, 1989).

27. See remarks by Congressman Benjamin Gilman, House Committee on Foreign Affairs, 3 Feb. 1993.

28. Carothers, *In the Name of Democracy;* on the activities of the NED, see its annual reports for the years 1988 to 1993. On the role of the NED in Chile during the plebiscite, see Tulchin and Varas, eds., *From Dictatorship to Democracy* (Boulder: Lynne Rienner, 1991); and Thomas E. Skidmore, *The Media and Politics in Latin America* (Baltimore: Johns Hopkins University Press, 1993).

29. See, for example, the Aspen Institute's *Convergence and Community*.

30. See hearings of the House Foreign Affairs Committee, 3 Feb. 1993.

31. Interview with Alexander Wilde, Washington Office on Latin America, 21 February 1992; also, Douglas W. Payne, "Latin America and the Politics of

Corruption," *Freedom Review* (January–February 1993); and the Stanley Foundation, *International Human Rights and US Foreign Policy* (Muscatine, IA: Stanley Foundation, 1992).

32. Porter, "Enterprise."

33. Ibid, p. 6.

34. John Williamson, "What Washington Means by Policy Reform," in Williamson, ed., *Latin American Adjustment: How Much Has Happened?* (Washington DC: Institute for International Economics, 1990).

35. The trip subsequently was postponed until December 1990.

36. Hakim, "Enterprise for the Americas Initiative."

37. See S. Weintraub, "Modeling the Industrial Effects of NAFTA," in Nora Lustig, Barry P. Bosworth, and Robert Z. Lawrence, eds., *North American Free Trade* (Washington, DC: Brookings Institution, 1992), pp. 109–132. Felix Peña, "Competitividad," and Roberto Bouzas, "US-Mercosur."

38. For a detailed discussion of this concept with reference to the Caribbean, see Tulchin, "The Formation of United States Policy in the Caribbean," *The Annals* (spring 1994).

39. Trade always has been considered more "natural" to US leaders than entangling alliances. See Felix Gilbert, *To the Farewell Address* (Princeton: Princeton University Press, 1961).

40. On the confusion in US foreign policy formulation, see the Stanley Foundation, *Global Changes and Institutional Transformation: Restructuring the Foreign Policymaking Process* (Muscatine, IA: Stanley Foundation, 1992).

41. See, especially, the work of several scholars at FLACSO, Chile—for example, Varas, "Global Transformations," and the project conducted jointly by FLACSO and the Woodrow Wilson Center that conducted national and regional seminars on the subject to encourage public debate. Another effort, in Argentina, is represented by Roberto Russell, ed., *La Política Exterior Argentina en el Nuevo Orden Mundial* (Buenos Aires: GEL, 1992).

42. Remarks by General Fernando Arancibia during the seminar, "Los dividendos de la paz," conducted by RIAL, Santiago, Chile, 25 Oct. 1990.

43. For a Bolivian lament by the minister of finance, see Jorge Quiroga, et al., " Reviewing Bolivia's Economic Transformation," Woodrow Wilson Center Latin American Program, working paper no. 201 (1992). On the restructuring programs, see Richard E. Feinberg and Valeriana Kallab, eds., *Adjustment Crisis in the Third World* (Washington DC: ODC, 1984); Howard Handelman and Werner Baer, eds., *Paying the Costs of Austerity in Latin America* (Boulder: Westview, 1989); and Nora Lustig, *Mexico: the Remaking of an Economy* (Washington DC: Brookings Institution, 1992).

44. Simon Teitel, ed., *Towards a New Development Strategy* (Baltimore: Johns Hopkins University Press, 1992); and Enrique Iglesias, *Reflections on the Development Process* (Baltimore: Johns Hopkins University Press, 1992); and Osvaldo Sunkel, "Alternate Development Models," manuscript in the possession of the author.

45. See, for example, the public discussion of a complaint by Terrence Todman, the US ambassador to Argentina, of corruption affecting a US firm attempting to do business in Argentina, *Clarín*, 23 March 1992; *Página 12*, 24 March 1992; and the scathing exposé published by Heracio Verbitsky, *Robo para la corona* (Buenos Aires: Planeta, 1992).

46. Simon Schwartzman, "Technology Transfer and the New Model of Economic Development," ms. in the possession of the author; and Gustav

Ranis, "International Migration and Foreign Assistance: Concepts and Application to the Philippines," manuscript in possession of the author; and Enrique Iglesias, *Reflections*.

47. Advocates of the reforms insisted equity would come eventually, through the "equity of the market," A. Alsogaray, "Va a ser resistencias," *La Nación*, 9 Dec. 1992; and, more generally, Felipe Larrain and Marcelo Selowsky, eds., *The Public Sector and the Latin American Crisis* (San Francisco: ICS, 1991). On the spread of poverty, see Samuel Morley, "Research on poverty in Latin America," manuscript study prepared for the World Bank, in the possession of the author.

48. On the Venezuelan case, see Tulchin and Gary Bland, *Venezuela: The Lessons of Democracy* (Boulder: Lynne Rienner, 1993). On the links between poverty and social tension, see John Walton, "Global and National Sources of Political Protest: Third World Responses to the Debt Crisis," *American Sociological Review* 55 (Dec. 1990); and Walton, "Debt Protest and the State in Latin America," in Susan Eckstein, ed., *Power and Popular Protest* (Berkeley: University of California Press, 1989).

49. Remarks ("not for attribution") by a senior Defense Department official at the conference, "Warriors in Peacetime: The Military and Democracy in Latin America, New Directions for U.S. Policy." (11–12 Dec. 1992). It is worth noting that this official indicated he considered the traditional concept of sovereignty to be "impractical" and that it was being replaced by a concept of "national integrity" in the definition of the conditions for "humanitarian intervention." For a Latin American view of shared security, see Francisco Rojas, "Toward a Hemispheric Regime of Shared Security," in Bruce Bagley, et al., eds., *The United States and Mexico: Economic Growth and Security in a Changing World Order* (Miami: University of Miami Press, 1993).

50. Nathaniel C. Nash, in the *New York Times*, 9 June 1991, iv, 2.

51. See V. P. Vaky and Heraldo Muñoz, *The Future of the Organization of American States* (New York: Twentieth Century Fund, 1993).

52. Monica Hirst and Carlos Rico, "Regional Security Perceptions in Latin America," Serie de Documentos e Informes de Investigacion (Buenos Aires: FLACSO, May 1992).

Index

171

About the Book

The essays in this volume constitute a careful, thoughtful analysis of the daunting problems that lie ahead for the nations of Latin America as they attempt to consolidate their democratic polities. Originally presented at a forum jointly organized by the Woodrow Wilson International Center for Scholars and the Olof Palme International Foundation, each essay has been thoroughly revised and brought up to date. The resulting book represents perhaps the first comprehensive survey in English of the linkages between democratic consolidation and economic reform in the region.

The authors are unanimous in cautioning against excessive optimism: the transition to democracy is not irrevocable, nor is economic liberalization by itself a panacea for all ills. Even under conditions of macroeconomic prosperity, they remind the reader, the preservation of democracy requires vigilance, patience, and hard work.

Joseph S. Tulchin is director and **Bernice Romero** is program associate of the Latin American Program, the Woodrow Wilson International Center for Scholars.